D0075683

Eric Hoffer

Twayne's United States Authors Series

Warren French, Editor

Indiana University, Indianapolis

TUSAS 425

"Common sense is genius dressed in its working clothes."
Ralph Waldo Emerson

ERIC HOFFER
Photograph © 1977 by George Knight

Eric Hoffer

By James T. Baker

Western Kentucky University

Twayne Publishers • Boston

Eric Hoffer

James T. Baker

Copyright © 1982 by G. K. Hall & Company
Published by Twayne Publishers
A Division of G. K. Hall & Company
70 Lincoln Street
Boston, Massachusetts 02111

Book Production by John Amburg

Book Design by Barbara Anderson

Printed on permanent/durable acid-free
paper and bound in The United States
of America.

Library of Congress Cataloging in Publication Data

Baker, James Thomas.
Eric Hoffer.

(Twayne's United States authors series ; TUSAS 425)
Bibliography: p. 142
Includes index.

1. Hoffer, Eric. 2. Social reformers—United States—Biography. 3. Labor and
laboring classes—United States—Biography. I. Title. II. Series.
HN64.B264   303.4'84 [B]   81–23760
ISBN 0–8057–7359–2   AACR2

For Margie Grant,
who is still
after all these years
the best of my teachers

Contents

About the Author

James T. Baker is a graduate of Baylor University (B.A., 1962) and Florida State University (Ph.D., 1968). He is presently professor of History and director of the Honors Program at Western Kentucky University.

Doctor Baker spent 1975 in Italy, where he studied art and intellectual history in Florence and Rome. In 1977 he was Fulbright Senior Lecturer in history at Seoul National University in Korea. Since 1979 he has coordinated his university's British Study Honors Program and in 1980 was awarded his university's highest honor for scholarship.

He is author of six books, including *Thomas Merton—Social Critic* (a study of the life and thought of the famed Trappist monk) and *A Southern Baptist in the White House* (a study of the religious personality of the thirty-ninth President of the United States). *Eric Hoffer* is the result of two years of research, which included a visit with Hoffer in San Francisco in late 1978.

Doctor Baker currently resides in Bowling Green, Kentucky, with his daughters Virginia and Elizabeth.

Preface

"That which is unique and worthwhile in us makes itself felt only in flashes. If we do not know how to catch and savor these flashes, we are without growth and without exhilaration" (*EH,* #1).[1]

It was over bratwurst and beer, in a German restaurant called Shroeder's in San Francisco, that Eric Hoffer told me how to write this book. "Write it with a light heart and with a smile on your face," he laughed. "I'm a freak. I never should have lived this long. I never should have written a famous book. I have nothing to prove to nobody. I am free to make a fool of myself three times a day." He meant what he said, and I have taken what he said (with a grain of salt) to heart.

Hoffer began his first and still best known book, *The True Believer,* with a line from his hero Montaigne: "All I say is by way of discourse, and nothing by way of advice. I should not speak so boldly if it were my due to be believed."[2] This is perhaps the key to understanding Hoffer and his marvelous little books. While he certainly wants to be read by as many people as possible, to have his "barbed" sentences catch and germinate in the minds of his readers, to serve as an example to those who desire to respond creatively to "ideas that dance," he does not speak with pontifical authority. He prefers to be a gadfly, a playful child, a passionately dispassionate observer of man and his world.

"If I can write a book, everyone should be able to write a book," he once told a college convocation.[3] "Our triviality is proportionate to the seriousness with which we take ourselves," he wrote in *Reflections on the Human Condition.*[4] And he was not displaying false modesty when he told a writer for *Life* magazine: "Tolstoy said your real worth is what you are divided by what you think you are. I find it very easy to keep the denominator small."[5] This sincere conviction of humility, which has helped Hoffer avoid the personal and social excesses of writers with more inflated egos, is demonstrated by his brevity. He appears almost as an intruder in print. His entire body of published writings would fill no more than one volume of the collected works of some thinkers. He has purposely chosen to publish only the distilled essence of a lifetime of rigorous study. He believes the public has better things to do than read any but the most finished of his writing.

This book, which will examine Hoffer's life and thought in more detail than either have been examined before, will be as brief—and we may hope half as polished—as one of Hoffer's own nine books. Like one of Hoffer's books, it can be read but not necessarily absorbed quickly. "Lying is a form of creativity; telling the truth is being only a reporter," Hoffer once told a class at Berkeley.[6] While this book claims to report accurately the major events and accomplishments of Hoffer's life, it does not claim absolute objectivity or disclaim interpretative creativity. It claims only to interpret the facts in the grand Hoffer manner and style.

For a man nearing eighty who believed he would die at forty and who has been threatening gastric cataclysm for two decades, Hoffer seems still in reasonably good health, despite a heart attack in 1977. But he is smaller physically now than he was in his prime, he requires more rest, and his mind has a tendency to wander. While he may live a good while longer, he is probably at the end of his active writing career. He will publish one more volume, a collection of the best of his past work—a "Hoffer Sampler," he likes to call it; but despite warnings that he plans to write a novel, we should expect no more major, original Hoffer works.

In his latest book, appropriately titled *Before the Sabbath* (1979), Hoffer says that as he finished *In Our Time* (1976) he felt he was scraping the bottom of the barrel. He found his reason unimpaired, his judgment still sound, his ability to tell sense from nonsense intact. He still loved to pursue unanswered questions; but he noticed that he was less alert, less interested in the world around him, less able to spurn the seductions of wishful thinking. So he decided to keep a journal, a "sluice box" he called it, to catch any last drops of essence from "a shrunken mind" the way he had once panned for gold in the California mountains.[7] This journal, *Before the Sabbath*,

proved that in his seventy-fourth year Hoffer's mind was still churn-
ing up some rich ore; but it also showed that the ore had not changed
in quality or color for a quarter century. He had said it all before,
in other words, of course, and in response to other historical circumstances; and it was all there was to be said. He was quick to
say that night at Shroeder's: "You don't need to ask me any questions,
really, because all I have to say, all I am, all I have said or will say,
it's in the books."

Hoffer and his nine original books form one of the richest veins
a student of philosophy, history, or sociology could hope to mine.
Blind from seven to fifteen, without formal education of any kind,
a self-taught philosopher specializing in "man the political animal,"
Hoffer has spent his adult life as a migrant farm laborer, a longshoreman, a sage without academic portfolio. Having read every
book the lending libraries of California could provide, having pursued fascinating questions with the tenacity of a bulldog, having
played hunches, captured brief flashes of insight, polished and re-
fined his notes, Hoffer has through sheer intellectual energy forged
a few lean sentences, then paragraphs, then essays, then books that
will live among the greatest of American letters. *The True Believer,
The Ordeal of Change,* and *First Things, Last Things*: these three books
alone would establish his reputation beyond detraction.

Stacy Cole, a mutual friend, the only disciple Hoffer has ever
tolerated, the man who will someday write the definitive Hoffer
biography, brought us together. Stacy, who cares for Hoffer the way
a son should care for his father, first attended the Hoffer seminars
at Berkeley (1964–72), where he collected on note cards a priceless
cache of Hoffer pronouncements on every subject from the Hebrew
God to the Russian *Sputnik*. Since Hoffer's retirement, first from
the waterfront and then from the university, Stacy has spent at least
one day a week in San Francisco, helping Hoffer answer his mail
and wash his clothes, sharing a meal with him at Tommy's Joynt,
discussing world affairs.

Stacy arranged for me to have dinner with Hoffer and his lady,
Lili, one night late in 1978. It was a sumptuous meal, spiced with
grand, noisy arguments between Hoffer and Lili about Hoffer's
tendency to stereotype races, nations, and individuals. "I see peo-

ple," Lili continually explained, a bit embarrassed by the raging battle, "while Eric sees types." From dinner at Shroeder's we moved to Lili's home, where she conducts an informal salon for the unending stream of people who come to the Haight-Ashbury looking for her man. Lili is a former California farm girl of Italian extraction (Fabilli was her maiden name), now a teacher of special education, the mother of the young man Hoffer calls his godson, and Hoffer's closest companion for a quarter century. Constantly engaged in one argument or another, it is evident to everyone that they love each other dearly.

Hoffer usually retires soon after nine each evening, but that night we all talked until two in the morning. Around ten our wide-ranging discussion was interrupted by a knock at Lili's door. "Jonathan!" Hoffer shouted as he saw a young man enter. "This is Jonathan," he explained as he embraced the thin, curly-haired boy. "He's an artist, a sculptor. He's doing me. He's a genius. He's made me one big head."

"It's supposed to be a bust, but it turned out to be just a head," the boy smiled, showing us photographs of the massive ball of clay that succeeds in capturing Hoffer's features while remaining a lump of earth, a natural object. "That's what I see when I look at him, one big head," he said innocently, his creativity surpassing his cognitive awareness.

"Now my job," Hoffer went on, "is to persuade some of my rich Oklahoma oil men friends to buy it and make Jonathan rich, the way a Jewish artist should be. I always bow before the shrine of creativity." This sent him into a long dissertation about the possibility of creating a coterie of Oklahoma Medici.

When after another four hours of high conversation on every subject from Father Adam to Richard Nixon we finally said goodbye to Hoffer at the door of his apartment house, near the waterfront where he worked and wrote five of his books, it was obvious that we had been in the presence of genius. He was perhaps past his prime, but a rich residue of his years of ferment still remained. His mind still gave off a potent, heady brew. Strong impressions remained with us as we headed out of the city Hoffer loves so dearly into the countryside where he once followed the crops:

1. There is his dispassionate passion, which has so thoroughly confused his readers from the beginning. His first reviewers, never having met Hoffer, never having heard him speak, labeled his polished, aphoristic prose icy. They were surprised, as was Eric Severeid, who admitted as much, to find him so emotional, so hot blooded, so loud and even vulgar. When Hoffer speaks he screws up his face, pounds his hands together, and shakes the earth with his bass voice. His writing is precise because he has spent such long hours tracking down information, "chewing" on the problem he has found so fascinating, writing and rewriting his hypotheses and conclusions; but the mind that forges such finely molded lines is fueled by a passionate love of knowledge.

2. There is his mind, still alert, still sharp, still able to recall almost every line of his published works verbatim. He admits that he has sent his only copy of each new manuscript to his publisher without fear of losing them because he could have rewritten each one from memory. His early blindness, his years of entertaining migrant laborers with his learning, his practice of having foreign sailors teach him passages from their native literature, many influences have trained his remarkable mind to retain everything that crosses its path. He speaks snatches of several languages, and he speaks each one without an accent. Ralph Lynn, a professor from Baylor University in Texas, tells about the night Hoffer entertained a gathering of scholars by quoting Psalm 104 first in English and then in flawless Hebrew before concluding with a catch in his voice: "That's the most beautiful passage in the whole goddam Bible."[8]

3. There is his gift for philosophy. Hoffer claims not to be a philosopher, not to understand philosophy;[9] and it is true that he is no abstract, obscure pedant, as some scholarly superstition would say a philosopher must be. But he is a true "lover of wisdom" who passionately pursues knowledge and finds sensual pleasure in the composition of clear, precise statements. It has been said that there are three kinds of creative minds. Small ones write of people, medium-sized ones write of events, and great ones write of ideas: thus the novelist, the historian, and the philosopher. Hoffer's is the great mind. His is the world of ideas. He even has the added talent of making ideas solid and plain to the common man.

Hoffer might indeed be called the common man's philosopher. He may well be, as some have suggested, the fulfillment of the dreams of man like Rousseau and Thoreau, who looked for the day when rustic philosophers would spring from the loins of the emerging lower classes. Once when a Berkeley student called Hoffer uncommon, he huffed, "Who says I'm not common? Because I read and write books? How would you know? How many common men have you known?"[10] He once told a questioner: "I know I have original ideas; I am intelligent, I can figure things out. But I believe everyone can."[11] He denies that he is a spokesman for the common man. He says he is the common man. He is certainly a walking example of Emerson's definition: "Common sense is genius dressed in its working clothes."

Hoffer offers his readers little hope, just courage. His experiences make him at times a bit gloomy, [12] but he believes man will survive if he has courage. Once when he was "on the bum" in southern California, he was picked up by a wealthy German candy maker near "the little German town" of Anaheim. The man scolded Hoffer for having no ambition and finished a little homily with a line from Goethe, "Without hope, all is lost." Hoffer suspected the accuracy of the quote because he thought that a man of Goethe's intelligence would know that a man can live without hope. In the Anaheim Public Library he discovered that Goethe had really said: "Without courage, all is lost" (EH, 15). Courage has given Hoffer the strength to write his books, the courage of the inquisitive case, the courage to follow questions to whatever answers they may give.

A personal word of thanks is in order to the following persons: to the members of the Faculty Research Committee at Western Kentucky University, William Stroube, chairman, for the funds that enabled me to meet with Hoffer and spend a summer on my study; to Stacy Cole for arranging that meeting; to Dick Troutman for his encouragement; and to Virginia Baker for her patience while I completed this highly rewarding task.

James T. Baker

Western Kentucky University

Chronology

Chapter One
The Private Years

The Public Broadcasting System's 1978 documentary on Hoffer's life and thought, which featured scenes of San Francisco, readings from Hoffer by Richard Basehart, and long reminiscences from Hoffer himself, was titled "Eric Hoffer: The Crowded Life," after Hoffer's aphorism: "It is the crowded life that is most easily remembered. A life full of turns, achievements, disappointments, surprises, and crises is a life full of landmarks" (*EH, #*20).[1] Hoffer's life, lived entirely in America, three-quarters of it in California, has been full of constant movement, agony and triumph, search and discovery, wonderfully crowded.

Hoffer plays down the importance of his life. "It is not important. It is not even interesting," he says. "Ideas are all that's important."[2] Fearing that his interpreters will dismiss his theories as merely the natural reactions to certain obvious stimuli, especially afraid that some pseudopsychological "Freudian" interpretation may do harm to his cherished convictions, he has consistently challenged his interviewers to take his books at face value, not to impose biographical data on them, not to confuse or diminish their message with references to his life.

We should respect Hoffer's wishes in this matter, but we must also admit that any philosophy isolated from the life that conceived and nurtured it to maturity is an orphan more easily misunderstood and abused than one whose parentage is clearly known. Far from "explaining away" Hoffer's thought, a good knowledge of his life gives it deeper meaning and makes it all the more relevant to his readers. This is perhaps more the case with Hoffer's life and thought than with other thinkers because he has so readily drawn from private experiences the principles that have inspired his philosophy.

1

Pundits from the various media, always on the prowl for neat epithets to describe men too complex to fit the usual categories, have called Hoffer a "literary stevedore" (*New Yorker*, 1951), a "dockside Montaigne" (*Time*, 1955), an "epigrammist on the water-front" (*Reporter*, 1957), a "secular preacher" (*Christian Century*, 1963), a "philosopher of the misfits" (*Time*, 1963), a "docker of philosophy" (*Life*, 1967), and a "blue-collar Plato" (*Newsweek*, 1967). While all but the last of these cute titles are more or less accurate, none of them really captures the man himself; and it is encouraging that in the last decade this waggish game has been abandoned. Hoffer has proven, even to journalists, that he is beyond classification. He is truly one of a kind. There has never been anyone like him, just as there has never before been a working class like the one from which he sprang; and his kind will not likely be seen again in the brave new world just dawning.

Those visiting San Francisco to meet Hoffer have tried with only moderate success to describe the physical appearance of the man. Margaret Anderson, who "discovered" Hoffer and prodded him to write for publication, compared him in his forties to a great friendly sheep dog, radiating constant good will. Norman Thomas, who visited him just after the appearance of *The True Believer,* when Hoffer was fifty, described him as a large, bald, thickset, muscular man, "a bit awkward, but in manner active and eager."[3] Calvin Tomkins, interviewing him fifteen years later, just before his retirement, found him still strong though a bit stooped, his large head too heavy for his powerful neck, his great bursts of laughter mocking his complaints of ill health (*EH,* 1). Tomkins was impressed, as have been all of Hoffer's visitors, with the resonance of his bass voice, still thickly laden with a German accent despite the fact that he was born in the Bronx and has spent nearly sixty of his nearly eighty years in California.

The best photographs of Hoffer, taken in 1967, at the time of his now famous television interview with Eric Severeid of CBS News, were made by San Francisco photographer George Knight. Hoffer, then sixty-five, was still robust, still the pensive but exuberant worker-philosopher, still enjoying the physical and intellectual prime he had held for thirty years. He was then, as he had been since the early 1930s, a charismatic figure, a potential social evangelist who had carefully chosen to observe events from a distance, to analyze them in the quiet of his bachelor apartment at night, to explain their meanings in a few short books.

Hoffer at seventy-nine—"pushing eighty," as he puts it—is somewhat diminished by time from the man he was at sixty-five. His clothes no longer fit as tightly, he dozes off between the high points of a conversation, and he seems to relish talking of his own death. Yet there is still about him a very vital spark, a fierce determination not to surrender to the ravages of age, a vivid awareness of the dynamics of events swirling about him, a young man's fascination with questions that puzzle the most profound of minds. He is still very much the inquisitive case.

In his latest book, *Before the Sabbath,* Hoffer speculates that life (everyone's, his own included) can be divided into multiples of thirteen. At thirteen one reaches puberty; at twenty-six the mind at last catches up with the body; at thirty-nine comes true maturity; at fifty-three the creative person finds his second wind; at sixty-five one retires from secular employment; at seventy-eight it is time to die.[4] Fortunately, Hoffer did not accurately predict his own death in the year following the summer of 1980; but his other thirteens worked right on schedule. For a man who discourages the study of his own life, Hoffer has left a wealth of detail for the construction of a rather complete brief biography.

Childhood and Youth: In the Nursery

"Man was shaped less by what he had to do than by what he did in playful moments. The ascent of man was enacted in something like an Eden playground rather than a desolate battlefield" (*EH,* #13).

Eric Hoffer was born on 26 July 1902, in the Bronx, to immigrants recently arrived from Alsatian Germany. His parents, along with a single woman from Bavaria named Martha Bauer, had arrived in New York only a short time before Hoffer was born. Hoffer has never known why they made such a dramatic move, and he says he is not interested in knowing. An anthropologist once told him of an Alsatian town full of Hoffers, probably his ancestral home, and

Hoffer promptly and proudly forgot its name. He shows no interest in his family's history.

He remembers his father as a quiet man with red hair. Father and son seem never to have been close. The elder Hoffer, a cabinetmaker, never had ready cash, but he was seldom unemployed, and the small family was comfortable. The father owned a good-sized library which he valued highly ("There's money in the cupboard," he often said), and Hoffer speculates that back in Germany he was probably considered the village intellectual, perhaps the village atheist.[5] When the boy cried, his father would let him play with his books; and this is how Hoffer learned not only to love the feel of books but also how to make various classifications. He would arrange them first by weight, then by size, then by color; and as an old man he would say, "I think this was the beginning of any capacity for generalization that I have."[6]

It may also have contributed to his early literacy. At five he could read both German and English, and he still thinks of five as the golden age. At five, he says, he was a genius—and has been in decline ever since. Maturity, he likes to say, is the successful return to the age of five, "to recapture the capacity for absorption, for learning, the tremendous hunger to master skills . . ." (*EH,* 7). Hoffer is among the few to reach such a maturity.

Hoffer remembers his mother as a small woman, very indulgent toward her strapping first-born son. In 1907, when he was still enjoying his golden age, Hoffer's mother was still carrying her big baby when she fell with him down a flight of stairs. A deep cleft in Hoffer's forehead still bears testimony to the fall (*EH,* 7). Two years later, whether due to the fall or to some unrelated illness, his mother died and Hoffer went blind. Hoffer suspects but is not sure that all these things were linked, physically and/or psychologically, but he dismisses it with a shrug: "We can remember minutely and precisely only the things which never really happened to us."[7] It was the beginning of a life that Hoffer would say broke every bone in his body but did not run over him.

From 1909–1917, from ages seven to fifteen, Hoffer was blind. He never attended school. He learned no trade. He was in the constant care of Martha Bauer, his father's friend, now his surrogate mother. He describes her as a large-breasted woman with a small head and big peasant's heart. She cooked for him, told him stories, encouraged him to make grand philosophical pronouncements, and slept in his bed. He says that during those eight years he and Martha were one.[8] He remembers this as a happy time, but he also remembers a great deal of pain: "I was racked by monstrous headaches. My childhood was a nightmare and its shadow still hovers in the back of my mind."[9] The rest of his life he would wake in the middle of the night afraid he was blind again. Only the first glow of dawn would still the fear.

Martha encouraged her little blind boy to talk. She made him speak English (obviously with her own accent) so that he would be able to succeed in the new country. She reminded him over and over again of each clever thing he said. As a result, "all my life I've had the feeling that what I think and what I say are worth remembering."[10] And Hoffer's experience has suggested to more than one observer a radical theory of education: that the creative child should first be taught to speak clearly, his confidence constantly reinforced by praise, and only much later be taught to read.[11] Hoffer's unique experience may indeed help to account for the precision of his writing, all of it composed orally before being written, and for his ability to recite verbatim long passages of his own work and that of almost every other writer he has studied in detail. To this day he keeps his eyes closed tightly when he gives his recitations, perhaps following a habit established during his blind years, or just afterward when he was unaccustomed to sight.

Martha Bauer also taught Hoffer that he would die young, as had all the men in his family, perhaps before his fortieth birthday. Hoffer believes this was a blessing. He says he spent his first forty years without a care, passing through life like a tourist.[12] It may well be significant that he settled down to a steady job and began writing for publication, began trying to make something of himself, only when he reached his fortieth year in reasonably good health. Medical science had and would help him survive the illnesses and dangerous periods of life that Martha had expected to take him away the way they had his ancestors. But Hoffer credits Martha with all his success in life. "If I am anything at all," he says, "it is due to Martha."[13]

In 1917, when Hoffer was fifteen, his sight returned—as mysteriously as it had left. He does not remember whether it returned slowly or quickly. Since the family was poor, there were no doctors to follow his progress and make a report. Hoffer supposes the blindness was due to some emotional blockage, probably caused by his mother's death, and that puberty's juices somehow unplugged it. Whatever the cause, the return of his sight brought about the greatest crisis of his life, greater than the one when he lost his sight eight years before. It separated him from his Martha (*EH*, 9).

As soon as he could see well enough, he began reading every book he could find every waking hour. He says he felt a terrific hunger for the printed word. He believes also that he may have been trying to ruin his eyes so that he could again be blind and secure with Martha. A secondhand bookstore near his home had just acquired the library of an auctioned estate, and Hoffer read the entire set book by book. The first one he remembers reading was Dostoevski's *The Idiot,* which he has reread many times, always fascinated by the Russian master's ability to establish such concrete scenes. He was originally attracted to the book by hearing his father complain about him while he was blind: "What can you do with an idiot child?" The book opened new worlds to him. He would pass on from novels to physical science to political theory; but he would always dream of the day when he could go off someplace and read thousands of novels.[14]

In 1919, perhaps because she no longer felt needed by the seventeen-year old boy buried in his books, perhaps because with the Great War over she had the freedom to fulfill a long-standing dream, Martha Bauer returned to Germany. Hoffer never heard from her again. For twenty years, he now says, he did not miss her ("how utterly callous"); but in later years he says he hardly passes a night without thinking of her, without remembering the taste of her food and the affection she gave him.[15]

In 1920 Hoffer's father died, still a relatively young man, of a stomach disorder. "He just did not get up one morning," Hoffer recalls. The burial society that handled the estate asked Hoffer what he wanted to do, and he told them he wanted to go to live in California. Much later he would explain:

I knew several things: One, that I didn't want to work in a factory; two, that I couldn't stand being dependent on the good graces of a boss; three, that I was going to stay poor; four, that I had to get out of New York. Logic told me that California was the poor man's country.[16]

In California, he fantasized, he could sleep outside the year round and pick oranges off the trees when he was hungry.

The burial society gave him about three hundred dollars and a one-way train ticket to Los Angeles. He carried all his earthly possessions, including the favorites among his father's books, in a wicker basket by his side. On the way across the country, he says, he was "Americanized." He saw his land for the first time, and he ate his first pancake. He landed on skid row in Los Angeles and stayed there ten years. "You might say I went straight from the nursery to the gutter," he remembers.[17] Skid row, he says, was for him like the Jordan River: he dived in and came alive. The almost breathtaking change of his circumstances would affect all his subsequent thinking. He would spend his life contemplating and describing change, its difficulties, its contributions to man's progress.[18]

The 1920s: On the Bum

Once in Los Angeles, Hoffer took a cheap room near the public library, paid three months' rent in advance, began to read, and waited for some sort of revelation. None came. When his money was gone, he sold his books, then his clothes, and finally just went hungry. On the fifth day without food, as he paused at a street corner to watch pigeons mating and for a few moments was so absorbed that he forgot about the burning hunger he had learned to endure, the revelation did come. Hunger was no worse than a toothache. It was to be avoided but not feared. He simply had to fight it. He marched into the nearest restaurant, got a full meal in exchange for an hour washing dishes, learned from a fellow dishwasher about an unemployment agency, and soon had a job loading pipe. He would never be idle again. He would for twenty more years be "on the bum," just one step ahead of hunger, but he would never starve.

He soon mastered the science of finding jobs. He learned where to sit in the unemployment lobby, what color book to carry to

attract attention, the kind of careless but willing smile to flash to
the dispatcher. He soon mastered the technique of making people,
bosses or buyers, like him, and of selling himself or any other
product. Once he proved so successful at selling citrus fruit door
to door ("I could sell a bucket of oranges to a statue.") that he quit
after the second day, frightened by the power he found he had over
simpler men and women (*EH,* 13). Despite his lifelong admiration
for "peddlers" and their place in the history of man's advance through
the ages, despite all his praise for the culturally conscious "Medici"
in every age, he realized quite early that selling required lying, a
primary form of corruption; and he knew then and ever afterward
that he was "the most corruptible man in the world" (*EH,* 13). For
others it might be all right, but for him it was poison. One of his
most cherished blessings is that he has remained free of greed.

This flight from peddling was the first of Hoffer's many escapes
from compromising or binding situations. Once a man named Farb-
stein, the owner of a pipeyard, did trap Hoffer, with kindness, for
over two years. Hoffer escaped only when the man mercifully died.
Another time he was lucky to escape an offer of perpetual employment from a wealthy farmer. Still another time, during the 1930s,
he would barely escape the wiles of a woman lawyer who wanted
to send him to school and make a professor of him. He came to
believe that the malice of trying to control others is what theologians
meant when they said man was possessed by Original Sin. He chose
to lead a life of solitary poverty and freedom from entangling alli-
ances—until at the age of forty-nine he met Lili Osborne.

In 1930, after a decade on skid row doing odd jobs in the Los
Angeles area, with the Great Depression closing in on him and the
entire American society, Hoffer decided to commit suicide. It was
a logical step. He expected to die soon anyway, and he thought this
might be the time to help nature along. He bought a vial of oxalic
acid, put it on his shelf, and sat down to read the Old Testament
until his meager savings ran out. He was so absorbed by his reading
that the reality of his impending death failed to touch him until
he one day spent his last dollar. Death, he has said, poses no threat
until it comes tomorrow. He took a streetcar to the ocean, took a
drink of the poison, discovered that he really did not want to die

after all, spat the offensive liquid out onto the sand, and began walking out of Los Angeles heading south. Skid row was his past; his future was the road.

It was then, as he followed the road toward a new life, a life still uncertain but at least exciting, that the German candymaker gave him a ride and quoted Goethe to him: *"Hofnung verloren, alles verloren."* When later in Anaheim, at the public library, he discovered what he had suspected, that Goethe had actually said, *Mut verloren, alles verloren* (see Preface), and knew he had a philosophy for his new life. He would live without *Hofnung* ("hope"), and he would; all he needed was *Mut* ("courage"), and that he knew he had.

The 1930s: In the Fields

Hoffer spent the entire decade of the 1930s in the fields with refugees from the Great Depression, the community of poverty now correctly called "Steinbeck's People." He moved up and down the Imperial Valley as a migrant farm laborer. He worked for the forestry service. He became, among other things, a master stone wall mason. He spent winters prospecting for gold around Nevada City near Lake Tahoe (*EH,* 17). He developed a style of life that made him say even thirty years later, "It has always seemed essential not to own more than I can pack on my back" (*EH,* 37). Each time he hit a new town after a long period of work in the fields or mountains, he would find a barber (preferably Japanese) to clean him up, buy new clothes, and rent a room halfway between the books (library) and the girls (brothel). He knew and visited every library and brothel along the railroad lines of California.

He admits to having been "terrifically lusty" in those days, "full of juices that got all bottled up" during the weeks of hard labor and isolation. He admits to having walked sixty miles round trip for female companionship. He always prided himself on coming in clean and on bringing the girls he visited candy, flowers, and sometimes small bags of gold.[19] He is contemptuous of Freud and Freudian interpretations of human sexuality. Of Freud he has said: "He grew up in a tight little community, Vienna, inside a tight Jewish community, and inside that community was a tighter unit, the Freud family." As for himself, "I grew up like a plant in the field. Nobody looked over my shoulder. Nobody expected anything of me." Copulation, he says, meant no more than urination. "I could make an ass of myself or go to the dogs any time I felt like it."[20] Yet he says he had nightmares, always the same ones, that he had no arms. It had nothing to do with sexual repression, he says; it was simply that he was afraid he would never write. "Now how the hell could Freud explain my nightmares?"[21]

Hoffer seems to have found only one enduring love during his years on the move. Her name was Helen. She was five years older than he, and she was a lawyer. Hoffer first saw her in the train station in Berkeley. Her beauty overcame his timidity; he walked up and introduced himself, and they became friends. Recognizing his potential, his natural gift for the physical sciences, she offered to pay for his education, make him a professor, and he ran away. "She wanted to throw a rope around me," he explains. He left her and never saw her again, but he admits that he is still haunted by her memory.[22]

It was in the 1930s, "my decade," he calls them, that Hoffer's reading, personal experiences, and world events at last began to merge toward creative formulation. "The Hitler decade," when Americans of German extraction were particularly sensitive to international events, when during his wanderings Hoffer discovered the writings of his French literary model Montaigne, was the period when Hoffer's fermenting mind began to produce its heady wine. "It colors my thinking and shapes my attitude toward events," he says of the 1930s. "I can never forget that one of the most gifted, best educated nations in the world, of its own free will, surrendered its fate into the hands of a maniac."[23]

Hoffer's understanding of history and his interpretation of the meaning of man's existence, like those of his ancient Hebrew mentors, developed while he was still a nomad, when as a tramp he felt most keenly his human estrangement from nature. The writing down of his observations, interpretations, and theories came later, when like the Hebrews he had settled down in a city and had the leisure and freedom from nature's necessities required for literary enterprise; but all the spadework was done on the open road and in the fields.

Most of what he learned, despite the fact that he read so widely, came from personal experiences. "My stretched mind," he remembers, "was exaggerating and fitting together slight happenings into fabulous, hilarious tales."[24] "I don't deal with the abstract," he once said. "My train of thought grew out of my experience . . . just the way a leaf on a branch grows out of a tree."[25] So much the better, for "the wisdom of others remains dull until it is writ over with our own blood."[26] His observations were those of a man on the outer fringes of organized society, a misfit as he puts it, one of the thousands of pieces of human debris swirling in the windstorms of those difficult days. Hoffer's relationship to the American and world scene was similar to the relationship of Alexis de Tocqueville, one of Hoffer's heroes, to the faded French aristocracy of the 1840s: "I am near enough to know it thoroughly," de Tocqueville said, "and far enough to judge it dispassionately."[27]

Being a misfit himself, living in the presence of other misfits, led to some of Hoffer's earliest and most profound discoveries. At one point he found himself living in a federally funded work camp near El Centro. His ever active mind took notice of the physical condition of his fellow workers. Hardly a man among them was free of some major disability or other. Unacceptable to polite, settled, or practical society, they had all drifted west to make new starts in a new land. "Tramps as pioneers? It seemed absurd," Hoffer would later muse over his slowly dawning idea. Yet it was true here, and perhaps it had always been true. Perhaps the reason we think of pioneers as heroes is that by going out into an unknown frontier where awkwardness is not a certain disadvantage, the misfit proves his own worth to himself and becomes someone important in a field untouched by men successful back in settled society. No wonder, Hoffer observed, Americans believe so firmly in human regeneration.[28]

The misfit could, under different circumstances, without the opportunity to prove himself, become an agent of destruction. He could become, as Hoffer would identify him, a true believer searching for a cause, a cause that would enslave him and his fellow men. Hoffer would always remember an Italian he met in the fields, a man who showed him great courtesy and companionship until Hoffer made the mistake of criticizing Mussolini. The man was so angered by Hoffer's malediction against a man who had given him his only real sense of pride that he refused ever to speak to Hoffer again.[29] The lesson was not lost on Hoffer. He saw how easily this man, like millions of uprooted, solitary misfits around the world, could be molded into cogs in some mindless mass movement, the very kind of movement Italians and Germans were joining in such frightening numbers. The Islamic term "true believer" came to mind, and Hoffer had a working hypothesis.

California itself was of course one of the best places on earth to study "true believers" because nearly everyone in California was a transplant of one sort or another, uprooted, blown away from familiar moorings, forced into a social system that promised him wonderful success but also threatened to destroy him if he made a wrong move. A recent description of this fascinating state by Lewis H. Lapham, himself a former San Franciscan, was just as true in the 1930s as today:

In California so many people are newly arrived (in almost all declentions of that phrase) that their anxieties . . . provide employment for a legion of dancing masters . . . who smile and hold up gilded mirrors as false and flattering as the grandiose facades with which their patrons adorn houses built to resemble a baroque chateau or a Spanish hacienda.[30]

People living in such a society, not then as wealthy as today but just as confusing, were perfect models for Hoffer's study of "man in transition." It is no wonder that California, like Asia Minor in the ancient world, would be the womb of America's twentieth-century religions.

It was during the 1930s, then, that Hoffer formulated his theories about man the political animal. What he discovered about the nature of man would keep him busy the rest of his life trying merely to describe this fascinating creature, the "unfinished animal."[31] "Some watch others to learn what to do," he has said, "and some watch others to learn what not to do."[32]

During his years in the fields he was "adopted" and treated as a relative by almost every ethnic group. He has always wanted to write "A Book of Kindnesses" to thank everyone who was nice to him during his years of poverty. Man is full of kindness, he says, because he is capable of compassion. On the other hand, man is capable of incredible evil because he is also malicious. He bares his teeth when he smiles, showing that pleasure was once joy at another man's suffering. Man builds up his fellow man just to see him fail to live up to expectations. Hoffer was once befriended by a small-town butcher who the month before had led an attack on a Jewish tailor; and he was once attacked and seriously wounded by a Mexican he had never seen before.[33] Such behavior inspired him to apply a common chemical formula to anthropology: "You had a corrosive called sodium, and some abomination called chloride. You put them together and it was the staff of life."[34]

Compassion and malice, both gleaming in the eye of man, make the human creature a mixed bag of conflicting drives and emotions. Man either creates or he destroys, depending upon his natural endowments and opportunities. This is what makes American man, for Hoffer, a unique specimen. American man has been given the first opportunity in fifty centuries of human history to prove what the common man can do. He has proven what he can do, and this has made him kind. How can you describe the American, Hoffer often asks, without mentioning kindness?

It is likely that Hoffer's observations about the nature and destiny of man, however accurate, however universal in application, would never have made the printed page and been shared with more than a handful of fellow tramps had Hoffer not been such an avid reader. He held a card from every library along his well-beaten trails, and he says he always got a sensual thrill every time he borrowed a library book to read.[35] He called his borrowing cards "credit cards," and he ran up an enormous bill. He seemed always to find just the book to help him solve the problem he was chewing on at the time, and for years he thought it was sheer luck until he came across Louis Pasteur's famous dictum: "Chance favors the prepared mind." Hoffer found what he was looking for because he was prepared to recognize it when he saw it.

The books Hoffer read to satisfy both his hunger for knowledge and his need for intellectual entertainment taught him how to capture, organize, and share his observations and theories. They helped him focus his energies and inspired him to write his own books. He

preferred French writers (in translation) to Americans and certainly
to Germans. He found the French clearer, more accurate, and less
cluttered with academic superstitions. He was once asked by a magazine to list the ten writers who had most influenced him. He did
not bother to answer the letter; but he did make a list, and he
shared it with me. The first five—Montaigne, Pascal, de Tocqueville, Renan, and Bergson—were French. The second five included
two Englishmen (H. G. Wells and Francis Bacon), the Swiss historian Burckhardt, the Russian novelist Dostoevski, and the Hebrew
Bible. There were no Americans and decidedly no Germans. "There
is no such thing as a German sentence," he has said; "there is a
German page." "The whole idea that anything profound has to be
dark, has to be abstruse and difficult, that is a German superstition."[36]

Of the French writers, Montaigne was from the start the most
influential, particularly in matters of literary style. Hoffer's story
of his discovery of Montaigne bears repeating:

Late in 1936 I was on my way to do some placer mining near Nevada
City, and I had a hunch I would get snow bound. I had to get something
to read, something that would last me for a long time. So I stopped over
in San Francisco to get a thick book. I did not care what the book was
about—history, theology, mathematics, farming, anything, so long as it
was thick, had small print and no pictures.[37]

Chance favored the prepared mind. At Lieberman's, a secondhand
bookstore on Market Street, he found a book with a thousand pages
of small print and no pictures. He paid the dollar price, put it in
his knapsack, and headed for the mountains. Only when he was well
along his road did he notice the title: *The Essays of Michel de
Montaigne.*

It was the Florio translation, which reads like Francis Bacon and
the King James Bible. Hoffer did indeed get snowbound. He read
the book through three times, finding references to himself on every
page, and the barbed sentences stuck in his mind. He went on to
quote Montaigne at every hobo convention for the next few years
and then to write his own reflections on the human condition in
Montaigne's style.

From Montaigne and Pascal (whom he discovered in a Monterey library) Hoffer learned his literary style. Their opinions were not all that superior to his own rough-hewn conjectures, and he recognized that he might one day stand beside them in prestige if he could learn to match their style. He began to fill notebook after notebook with sentence upon sentence, learning how to make his thoughts concrete and clear, and catch the residue in a few precious sentences (*EH,*27). He would explain his process to Margaret Anderson in a letter:

My writing is done in railroad yards while waiting for a freight, in the fields while waiting for a truck, and at noon after lunch. Towns are too distracting. Now and then I take a day off "to put myself in order." I go through the notes, pick and discard.[38]

His mind, always active, had to have something to chew. He was in training to be a writer.

In 1939, after writing a couple of still unpublished novels and a musical comedy for a federal work gang in El Centro (which he left town without seeing),[39] Hoffer wrote an article on the subject of undesirables and sent it to a magazine called *Common Ground.* This publication, designed by the Common Council for American Unity to help interpret America to the foreign born and vice versa, had so completely met with Hoffer's approval that he honored it with his first literary offering. He found his first offering, as have so many great writers, rejected.

Common Ground could not publish his article-in-the-form-of-a-letter, Associate Editor Margaret Anderson wrote him; but she had sent it to Eugene Saxon at Harper and Row, and Saxon had suggested that Hoffer write his autobiography for publication. Hoffer rejected the idea, mumbling that he cared little for "personal" writing; but over the next ten years, as he settled down to work on the waterfront, he continued to receive letters from Ms. Anderson, encouraging him to write. He would later give her credit on the dedication page for inspiring him to write *The True Believer.* Margaret Anderson's name would now appear second in the short list of women who helped make Eric Hoffer. The third name would be Lili Osborne.

The 1940s: On the Waterfront

The advent of World War II galvanized Hoffer's resolve and changed his way of life. Late in 1941 he volunteered for military service, but was rejected because of a hernia that would require several operations in the coming years. Early in 1942, after casting about for the "hardest work available" to aid the war effort, he joined the International Longshoreman's and Warehouseman's Union (ILWU) and settled down to work on the waterfront in San Francisco. He would never again follow the road.

He rented a tiny apartment on McAllister Street (where he would live sixteen years) and bought a phonograph so that he could listen to the Beethoven he remembered from his childhood when his father would take him to concerts in New York. The bare apartment had room only for a bed and books and a flat board laid across two chairs for a writing table. There he would write *The True Believer,* copying it out from notes he "read from the cracks" in the ceiling and others preserved in his battered notebooks. Lili Osborne still cheerfully exhibits for guests the warped board, complete with coffee stain circles and abbreviated reminders, on which one of this century's most original English-language books was composed.

Harry Bridges, the tough, pro-Soviet, anti-Nazi head of the ILWU, permitted no strikes along the waterfront until the Third Reich fell in 1945; and except for a nine-month stay in the hospital in 1943 when a five-ton crate fell and sliced off his right thumb, Hoffer worked with hardly a break. When bone from a rib and skin from a thigh gave him a new thumb, in the same length of time it takes to conceive and deliver a baby, he went right back to work. He loved the waterfront. He admired and still admires Bridges personally and tolerated his political opinions; and he never ran for union office or opposed the organized hierarchy. He worked when he wanted to work, mostly at night, and spent his free time reading and writing. "It's like being on the bum in one place," he described his new life. "Some of my most original thoughts come to me while I work," he would later say. "If you can work, keep up a conversation and in the back of your mind compose sentences, it is a glorious feeling."[40]

His fellow workers, whom he found wonderfully kind and intelligent men, quite ingenious and needing little supervision, indulged Hoffer's eccentricities, calling him "professor," laughing when he went off to read during breaks, enjoying his boisterous banter as he worked and "composed sentences in the back of my mind on company time." He was friendly to all the men, but he carefully avoided making close friends, and he never had a steady partner. He chose "dull" work, chewed on problems and composed sentences with the "other side" of his brain, added crumb to crumb, and slowly turned vague theories into concrete assertions.[41] It was for Hoffer a grand time.

Living in one place, following a steady if eccentric routine, free of the demands of the seasons (the "iron laws of nature"), Hoffer's horizons expanded and his understanding of social dynamics deepened. Much he learned came from his fellow workers, who would never know their contribution to American letters because they would never read Hoffer's books.

A black worker who happened also to be a preacher helped him compose "the only poetic section" of *The True Believer,* the part titled "Things Which Are Not."[42] A clumsy partner who could not make himself stay with his own job long enough to finish it but who was always wandering off to help others made Hoffer see that pioneers are essentially awkward people who find acceptance only when they try to do something no one has done before (*EH,*31). An ad hoc collection of men sharing dinner by a forklift taught Hoffer that to love one's neighbor one must first love himself, that one does treat his neighbor as he treats himself, the thesis of an article on "Brotherhood" he was writing for the *New York Times.*[43]

It was also on the waterfront that Hoffer first met the prototype of the industrial age's intellectual. There were several such men about him, educated men working as industrial laborers in order to radicalize the workers, dreaming of a utopia run by an elite corps that knew what was best for everyone else. The intellectual who would have perhaps the most effect on Hoffer's life was Selden Osborne. Osborne, a roommate of educator Clark Kerr at Stanford, had brought to the waterfront, along with his Master of Arts degree, a plan for proletarian reform. He and Hoffer, ideological enemies from the start, would share a career and the love of a woman.

During his first days on the waterfront, Hoffer came to love Golden Gate Park; and once a week for the next thirty years he would take a leisurely five-mile walk from its top to its bottom. He would usually start off puzzling over some question or other, chew on it as he walked, and at the bottom sit down and write out his solution. He loved the park because, as he says, it was completely man-made. Nature as he had known it in the fields was an enemy; here, carefully cultivated and controlled, it was a friend. He could better understand the Romantic movement of the last century when he strolled in an environment much like Europe, where the movement began, than when he trudged through hostile North American wildernesses. He mused over the strange phenomenon of American college students, inspired by Wordsworth, going off into the California mountains to make love and coming home with poison ivy.

All through the 1940s, as he worked, Hoffer was writing *The True Believer.* Driven by an inner compulsion to write like the French analysts, by Margaret Anderson's confidence in him, by the spiraling world events that confirmed so many of his theories and explained many of his puzzles, he spent long hours at his plywood plank organizing his thoughts. "I tried to explain Hitler," he once said, "and one day I had a book." It was not quite that simple, of course, but generally that was his process.

The actual composition of *The True Believer,* after its outline was formed, was done during two three-month postwar strikes, one in 1946 and one in 1948. "I had seen the world like a dead horse with its belly ripped open," he said. "In the late 40's, the scholars tried to sew up that belly and forget the putrification inside. I couldn't forget."[44] He wrote his book in complete intellectual isolation, discussing it in disguised forms only with his fellow dock workers. It was written backward. All of the ideas were his own; but he knew publishers would want him to cite "authorities," and so he found them. He looked until he found an "authority" who agreed with each of his theories, then recast their actual words in his own language, often taking them beyond their original potential. Unlike writers who string together the ideas of other men until they have a book, Hoffer wrote his own book and then humbly found "authorities" to give it prestige. He would never have to do this again.

The True Believer offered answers to the major questions troubling the postwar generation:

1. What makes mass movements appealing to so many people?
2. What kind of people are attracted to these mass movements?
3. What kind of men inspire, lead, and then consolidate mass movements?
4. What common characteristics do mass movements, good and bad, share?

"It's divided up in sections," Hoffer explained, "and you can master one section at a time. . . . Whenever I had the least doubt that I might not have made myself clear I repeated, again and again, like a screw that repeats itself but each time goes a little deeper."[45] The result of his labor, his willingness to wrestle with the great issues of modern society, his long years of perfecting his skills, was a masterpiece.

In 1948 Hoffer mailed an introduction and an outline (in longhand) to Margaret Anderson, who relayed it to Elizabeth Lawrence at Harper and Row. The response was favorable. In 1949 he had the lady at the local candy store wrap the entire handwritten manuscript, mailed it to Ms. Anderson with a hundred dollars, and asked her to have it typed and submitted for publication. (A later fantasy had him looking up Harper and Row's address in the library and sending the handwritten draft directly to them.[46]) Sometime the next year, after he had long since given up hoping for a reply, a telegram was slipped under his door. Thinking it was an advertisement, he almost threw it away before realizing it was telling him that his book would be published.

The True Believer sold extremely well for a book of its kind, and for thirty years Hoffer has continued loyally to send Harper and Row his manuscripts. Elizabeth Lawrence was his first editor, then Cass Canfield, and now Corona Machemer. Harper and Row has not always advertised his books well, and they have often done a rather

poor job of keeping them in print; but Hoffer is still fiercely loyal
to them. He credits them with giving him the chance he might not
otherwise have had to get his ideas before the public; and besides,
he says, he is not a greedy man. "Count your blessings," he advises
Lili.

Because Hoffer published his first book at the age of forty-nine
and was "discovered" by national televison at the age of sixty-five,
he will always seem to the public an older man, just as many famous
poets will be remembered, because of early deaths, as younger men.
Hoffer was of course once a young man, and he says it is "too bad
you didn't know me then." His early gifts were for math and physics.
He was able, by his own account, to skip whole chapters of the
books he used to teach himself the most complicated intricacies of
these fields because the material was so evident to him. But he
carefully avoided a professional career in these areas just as he kept
no record of the music and made no effort to publish the fiction he
wrote during his middle years; and we are left to judge him solely
on his later work—all of it concerned with man the social and
political animal. Hoffer will always remain a great *older* mind.

There is no reason for mourning in this. Genius comes at different
ages for different disciplines. The abstract sciences such as mathematics and music are open (and on the more spontaneous levels open
only) to young minds. If genius in such fields has not appeared by
the late twenties, it likely will not appear. The more creative disciplines, literature and the arts, while they are open to younger and
older minds, seem best suited to people in their middle years. Minds
between thirty and fifty, still spontaneous but more experienced,
can respond creatively in ways younger and older minds cannot. But
it is only the older mind, the mind that was once spontaneous and
once creative, and still is both, that can satisfy the demands of
philosophy. Old age is the time to make pronouncements. An older
mind is either a sage's or a fool's, depending upon its learning and
its openness to new truth, and only an older mind can be a true
philosopher's.

Whatever gifts he may have had as a young and a middle-aged
man, Hoffer was meant all along for philosophy. This is why he
had to wait longer than most men for his greatest powers to ripen.

He was what educators call a late starter. Considering what he has accomplished, this is not at all to be regretted. A. S. Neill, founder of the controversial but much-admired experimental school Summerhill, once wrote in his usually wise manner, "I like to meet the man who at the age of fifty-three says he doesn't quite know what he is to be in life."[47] It is likely that Hoffer's mind, despite an early raw genius for the physical sciences, despite his later attraction to literature and the arts, was from the first meant for social criticism. He is one of those rare men who mature late enough that even their mature work reflects a child's fascination with the kind of questions that make a philosopher's observations worthy of posterity.

Chapter Two
The Public Years

It is always a bit risky to identify one particular year as the most decisive or important in a man's life; but as a turning point, when Hoffer became a celebrated writer, when he met the woman he would love the rest of his life, 1951 may have been Hoffer's year. In 1951 he saw the first copy of *The True Believer* and met Lili Osborne.

The 1950s: Dockside Montaigne

The True Believer, which spread the name Eric Hoffer and Eric Hoffer's story through the American literary community, was dedicated to Margaret Anderson, "without whose goading finger which reached me across a continent this book would not have been written." The dedication was structured poetically, and it represented Hoffer's deepest sentiments, for he once wistfuly remarked, "If I had lived with that woman, I would have written more."[1]

The term "true believer" had its origin in Islamic history and originally referred to the fanatically devoted religious fundamentalist who prefers purity to peace. While Hoffer did not coin the term, he did give it its secular, universal meaning and usage. Hoffer's "true believer" is the isolated, insecure person anywhere, at any time, who gives himself without reservation to any movement that promises his life meaning through action. The true believer, Hoffer wrote, "is everywhere on the march, and both by converting and antagonizing he is shaping the world in his own image."[2] Hoffer's thesis, which he would restate and expand in later books, was that this true believer is ripe for conversion to a grand cause because of his frustration with a life spoiled beyond the usual sources of hope. He is therefore ready to sacrifice his spoiled self, the spoiled society around him, this present spoiled time for a cause that saves him from meaninglessness and gives him a place in a movement dedicated to a new society in a new age.

Hoffer deals not just with his true believer (both leader and follower) but also with the common characteristics of various mass movements that attract him. They all generate fanaticism, encourage intolerance, give fervent hope, provide united action, and elevate to the level of heroism the willingness to die. They all release, capture, and channel a tremendous flow of energy from their fanatic converts to their utopian causes. They all demand blind faith and singlehearted allegiance to causes so "holy" they justify any type of behavior in their converts. They draw their followers from the same frustrated type of men: those searching for a cause to which they can sacrifice a spoiled present for a glorious future. "However different the holy causes people die for," Hoffer concludes, "they perhaps die basically for the same thing."[3]

The radical Nazi, the radical Communist, the radical Moslem or Christian, all quite different, are motivated by the same drives, led by the same sort of men, and follow movements that display the same social dynamics. Hoffer was careful to point out that all such mass movements do not have the same long-range effects. Quite simply, some are good and some are bad. The tomato and the nightshade are both of the taxonomical family *Solanaceae,* yet they have opposite effects on the man who tries to eat them.

Hoffer's main concern in the book is the active phase of the mass movement, the phase dominated by the true believer, "the man of fanatical faith who is ready to sacrifice his life for a holy cause." Neither the fact that Hoffer's model of the fanatic leader does not quite fit any single mass-movement leader nor the fact that his followers are pictured as so stereotypically sick detracts from Hoffer's skillful portrayal of the genesis and destiny of this world's true believers. *The True Believer,* though weakened in places by a new author's tendency to "perhaps" and "would seem" away some of his authority, pronounces its creator a grand master of social and political and psychological analysis.

Reviews of *The True Believer* were highly and consistently favorable, though hindsight proves that all of its reviewers did not fully catch all its implications. Richard Rovere, writing for the *New Yorker,* called it a "work of almost pure celebration and intuition." Hoffer, he concluded, was "a born generalizer, with a mind that inclines to the wry epigram and the icy aphorism." This feeling that the book was "coldly" precise was widespread, for Orville Prescott of the *New York Times* said it "glitters with icy wit."[4] This impression of Hoffer's writings continued for three more books and fifteen more years. S. K. Overbeck, reviewing *The Temper of Our Time* for *Newsweek* in 1967 called even that somewhat intemperate book "cool, glittering, diamond hard."[5] The reviewing establishment sometimes has a difficult time surpassing its own first impressions.

Perhaps it was hard to catch Hoffer's tone without meeting him. Eric Severeid, during his famous Hoffer interview for CBS in 1967, expressed surprise at finding the "icy" philosopher so bombastic, so emotional. Calvin Tomkins, who had interviewed Hoffer earlier that year for the *New Yorker,* had already expressed surprise at the "enormous difference between the dispassionate, somewhat icy tone of his writings and the intensely personal fervor of his speeches. . . ."[6] Only Garry Wills, reviewing *The Ordeal of Change* for *National Review* in 1963, had been able to penetrate the Hoffer mystique. He could tell from Hoffer's attitudes that he was at heart a romantic, and he had guessed without having met him that he was a man of great emotional intensity.[7]

Only in the 1960s, when Hoffer's increasingly hostile attacks on "intellectuals" had dampened liberal enthusiasm for him, did a harsh criticism of *The True Believer* surface. Joseph Featherstone, reviewing *The Temper of Our Time* for *New Republic,* referred back to Hoffer's first attempt to deal with this age of mass ideologies, *The True Believer,* which he said was a failure because Hoffer could not identify with his subject. Having no historical imagination, Featherstone said, in a decade when fanatic liberal causes were in vogue, Hoffer had pleased the Whiggish Eisenhower 1950s by branding all protesters sick cranks led by demoniacs.[8] More such liberal criticism would follow.

It is true, of course, *The True Believer*'s best "reviewer" was the leader of the Whiggish Fifties, President Eisenhower himself. Ike read the book in 1952, gave copies to his friends, and encouraged them to get acquainted with Eric Hoffer. *Look* magazine ran a feature on Hoffer in 1956, calling him "Ike's Favorite Author," and Hoffer became known, for better or worse, as the man Ike liked. Hoffer, who would use Eisenhower as the example that America could get along fine without a great leader, was embarrassed by his dubious distinction. "It proved to me something I always knew," he said, "which is that this is the kind of book that any child can read."[9]

1951 was also the year that Hoffer met his Lili. Lili's husband, Selden, one of the "intellectuals" on the waterfront, had met Hoffer and made friends with him, although as Hoffer once said, "It is a miracle that we understand each other when we say hello." Selden was a university graduate, a radical, a dedicated reformer without personal charm, usually depressed because of the failure of his various schemes. Hoffer thought Selden would have made a good Unitarian minister. He considered him a do-gooder, potentially dangerous if inept, and certainly out of place on the docks. But they were both sufficiently well read to argue, and Selden finally invited the fascinating rough genius home for dinner.

Hoffer called Selden's house to make the arrangements, and Selden's wife, Lili, answered. Lili, whose family had come from the Abruzzi region of Italy to a farm in California, knew when she heard Hoffer's voice that he was a paisano. There had always been a stray, foreign-born uncle or two about her father's farm, and she knew how to make them feel wanted. To make a very long story short, Hoffer and Lili fell in love. Selden and Lili, only partially due to Hoffer's intrusion, would eventually separate and divorce. Hoffer would help Lili buy a house on Clayton Street. He would ask her to marry him. She would refuse because she knew how miserable he would be tied down, but she would promise to be a wife to him in everything but name. She would give his latter years most of their comfort and joy.

Lili has had her own life during her years with Hoffer. She has taught retarded children in the Redwood City area. She has raised the family she began with Selden. She has fought with Hoffer over his tendency to stereotype people, particularly Italians, in what she calls a typically Teutonic manner. She has waged a losing battle to get Hoffer to demand more money from Harper and Row for his books. She has carefully stored away Hoffer's manuscripts, published and unpublished, despite the fact that Hoffer is always after her to make a bonfire of the whole lot.

The Osbornes already had a daughter (Tonia, born 1946) and a son (Steven, born 1949) when Hoffer entered the picture. The daughter, who suffered from epilepsy, never accepted Hoffer, eventually moved away, and died in New York City in 1963. The son, who now lives in Pennsylvania, studied at Berkeley and served in the Peace Corps in Morocco from 1969–71 and considers Hoffer a member of the family. In 1956 Lili was pregnant again. Hoffer predicted she would have a boy, that she would name him Eric, and that he would be the boy's grandfather. He was right on at least two of the counts. Hoffer denies that young Eric is his son, though the boy believes he is, but Hoffer has spent great time, money, and mental anguish to make the boy a useful citizen. He has had, by his own assessment, only limited success.

"For the first time in my life," Hoffer told Calvin Tomkins in 1967, "I have become attached to two people—the mother and my grandson. And I will never abandon these two people, even if it kills me."[10] Hoffer's journals make young Eric the central figure of his later years. He worries that the boy will be lazy, that he will take to drugs, that he will run away and waste his time. Yet he admits that young Eric (his godson) reminds him of himself at an early age, and he acknowledges that we consider brittle the things we love most. In point of fact, young Eric, now essentially estranged from Eric and Lili and living in Alaska, is very much the young Eric Hoffer.

In 1955 Hoffer's second book, *The Passionate State of Mind,* appeared. It was dedicated to his editor Elizabeth Lawrence. In its review *Time* magazine called its "pink-faced, horny handed" author a "Dockside Montaigne" and attributed to him a knack for "neat 17th century-style brooding on 20th century problems."[11] *The Passionate State of Mind* is not a book like *The True Believer.* It is a collection of 280 aphorisms, some as long as a page, some hardly more than one line, gleaned from Hoffer's pile of notebooks. A few are somewhat fatuous, but most are penetrating and stimulating. Taken together and rearranged a bit, they probe incisively the psyche of the true believer and go on to analyze the personality of the true believer's opposite number, the creative individual.

The artist and the revolutionary, Hoffer wrote, are inspired by the same personal dissatisfaction. The passion of the revolutionary is simply his lack of creative skills, for "where there is the necessary technical skills to move mountains, there is no need for the faith that moves mountains." The artist, the gifted creator, works without high passion, deriving satisfaction from a job well and smoothly done. He does not raise his voice the way the untalented do because "our impulse to persuade others is strongest when we have to persuade ourselves."[12] Again Hoffer, though maddening in his tendency to stereotype, goes to the heart of human dynamics and comes up with a provocative hypothesis.

The Passionate State of Mind, whose title has inaccurately been used to describe Hoffer's own personality, is not a book to be read quickly. The 280 aphorisms are to be read singly or in small clumps, turned over in the mind, tested in conversation, discarded or retained for further thought depending on individual merit. The best of them will catch and germinate in the reader's mind to produce thoughts far beyond the original intention of the aphorism. They are, shall we say, the sayings of a political guru.

By 1958 Hoffer was busy at work on a new book, one that would eventually rival *The True Believer.* It would eventually be published in 1963 under the title *The Ordeal of Change;* but in 1958 it was giving Hoffer fits. It had started out as a book on "men of words," but it had of its own will become a book on change. Maybe it was two books, Hoffer thought, and maybe not. He could not think for the noise around him. What had once been a poor white neighborhood was becoming increasingly black, and in his own house there was "a whorehouse beneath me and a madhouse above." He hated to move, as he had once hated leaving certain work camps where he had ideas stuffed into the cracks in the ceilings. He loved his apartment on McAllister Street. He had lived there for sixteen years. Only once had he considered moving, in 1952 when *The True Believer*'s success seduced him into thinking he should live more like a rich writer, and his first royalty check disabused him of such grand notions. Now he was being forced out.

He found a new apartment on Clay Street, among quiet Chinese people. He would be happy there until several years later when the older families began giving way to newer "Hong Kong" Chinese people with noisy children. Then he would throw bottles at them and curse them in Chinese, and the police would come; and eventually he would move to a high-rise apartment in Davis Court. But Clay Street was at first just what he wanted. Calvin Tomkins found his second-floor apartment there in 1967 Spartan to the extreme but just the way a Hoffer needed it. A bookcase full of secondhand copies of every type book, a table covered with cards and notebooks, another table with a dictionary and paper for writing, two straight chairs, and a bed that folded into a closet.[13] In this setting he would write *The Ordeal of Change.*

Moving was traumatic for Hoffer, after sixteen years in one place, and so was his temporary writing block; but the result of all his anxiety was one of his most interesting books, a diary he kept between 1 June 1958 and 21 May 1959 entitled *Working and Thinking on the Waterfront.* He filled seven small notebooks during those hard months, and then he put the diary away when he found himself making progress once again on his manuscript. It was seven years before he found these notebooks, shared them with Lili, and they agreed to offer them for publication. *Working and Thinking on the Waterfront* would eventually appear in 1969, when it was ten years old.

It is a delightful book, full of trips with Lili and young Eric, Hoffer's personal feelings about "intellectuals" on the docks and around the world, his comments on every major news event during the year. It shows him bored with union meetings, impatient with the complaints of Third World politicians, and fighting mad at mendacious Russians. It shows how Hoffer's mind added crumb to crumb until he had an essay. Ross Mackenzie, who reviewed the book for *National Review,* said that more than any of his books this one demonstrated Hoffer's genius for searching out the causes behind social and political events. It established Hoffer as a true seeker after truth.[14]

The 1960s: Docker of Philosophy

The 1960s, with their polarities, their stretching, their confusion, released a tremendous flow of American energy. This energy fueled hundreds of large and small movements, some positive and creative and uplifting, others negative and destructive and degrading. Hoffer was for the first time caught up in the major news events of the time. Living as he did in San Francisco, teaching at Berkeley, now a nationally known figure, he could not avoid the pain that decade inflicted.

In 1960, as if to inaugurate a decade of trial, the ILWU concluded a new labor contract with the Pacific Maritime Association under which over a period of years machines would gradually replace human energy on the waterfront. As the contract began effecting change, as men became less necessary, Hoffer began to stir. Immersed already in writing his book on change, he feared that automation was about to produce a whole army of skilled and semiskilled workers who in their boredom could be molded into a mass movement of true believers by frustrated men of words. For the first time he began accepting invitations to lecture, and he found his oratorical powers frightening. Lili Osborne, who often accompanied him and heard many of his speeches, described the relationship Hoffer established with audiences as being like "lovemaking in public." Hoffer himself, realizing perhaps for the first time how much he was like the fanatic true believing leaders of mass movements, admitted, "I have always had it in me to be a fanatic."[15]

Many of his acquaintances say that Hoffer, with his oratorical skills, could have led a social revolution in the 1930s or been a labor leader in the 1940s and 1950s or been a successful candidate for public office in the 1960s. Hoffer counters that he would never have been any of those things because he never hungered for power, because he never held a grudge against anyone. The quest for power, he says, the hunger to lead a cause, is born of a passion to punish enemies, to right wrongs by stripping and beating those who have done one wrong. Once on a freight train, he says, he could have crushed a small Mexican who for no reason had earlier stabbed him in the leg, and he simply turned away in disgust.[16] No grudges, no power, no movements.

Hoffer's fear of automation slowly waned as he watched it take over the docks. He began to see it not as an evil but as potentially a good thing for the workers. It could, he wrote in *The Temper of Our Time* (1967), if used wisely and efficiently, save the men a lot of backbreaking labor; and it could provide some among them with the leisure to create a new proletarian golden age. Man, he would come to believe, was at last fighting his way back to the gates of Eden.

In 1963 appeared Hoffer's third book, *The Ordeal of Change,* dedicated to "Lili and all the Osbornes." A book of sixteen essays in which Hoffer's personal experiences and observations, without apology for their originality, are projected onto national and world screens, *The Ordeal of Change* takes Hoffer's pursuit of true believers into the postwar era of spiraling social change and the emergence of three distinct and estranged worlds. In its clarity, its originality, and its provocativeness it is perhaps Hoffer's best book. Hoffer agrees.

The Ordeal of Change is concerned with human nature, with the effects of change on human nature, with the role of "undesirables" created by change, and with the benefits (therapeutic, practical) of work on men dealing with change. Written essentially in the 1950s, it speaks directly to the problems of the 1960s. It seems to prove Hoffer's argument: "Listen to what I am saying, then wait ten years and you will hear everyone saying it."[17]

Reviewers were unanimous in their praise of *The Ordeal of Change.* It was hailed as one of the few contemporary books with any chance of influencing the course of human history. It was said to be one of those rare books that make the reader face up to the carelessness with which he holds certain assumptions so easily proven false. *Time* magazine, dubbing Hoffer "Philosopher of the Misfits," called *Ordeal*'s author the dream of the Romantics come true: a philosopher had sprung from the masses.[18] Not only had Hoffer here demonstrated the threat to the common man of "intellectuals" who would champion the masses in order to be their masters, but he had also constructed perhaps the first common man's philosophy of history.

Christian Century's Penultimate column nominated the author of *The Ordeal of Change* as "our candidate least likely to be invited to a D.A.R. meeting" as guest speaker because he would probably tell the good ladies that America was made great by misfits. Penultimate also said that with his wide literary background, his magnificent generalizations so free of prissy academic inhibitions, and his pithy phrases Hoffer would make a great lay preacher.[19]

Garry Wills, then still with *National Reveiw*, congratulated Hoffer on having survived the cruel fate of having his prose understood by Eisenhower before proceeding to penetrate Hoffer's "icy" facade. Hoffer, Wills was the first to say, was at heart a Romantic. In the nineteenth century, he said, the "Sunday romantics" went to lectures while the real ones died at Missolonghi; and now the Sunday variety play "sit-in" while the real ones go to their jobs on the docks.[20]

In 1964 Selden Osborne, whose rivalry with Hoffer for Lili's attention seemed never to have dampened his admiration for Hoffer the philosopher, joined with Professor Norman Jacobson in persuading Chancellor Clark Kerr to invite Hoffer to teach at the University of California at Berkeley. Hoffer, agreeing to become "gossipper-in-residence,"[21] was named "Resource Professor of Political Science." From 1964 to 1972, at a salary in the range of $16,000 a year, Hoffer gave a handful of annual public lectures and from two until five o'clock each Wednesday held an open seminar for students, teachers, and anyone else who wanted to come to see him in the upper reaches of Barrows Hall. "You have to be a genuine detective to find me," he joked; but he was never without academic companions.[22]

From the first he felt ill at ease with undergraduates and even the younger graduate students. They seemed to him terribly spoiled, demanding knowledge and power without working to earn either of them, "fighting straw battles against a straw enemy, which is the university that shelters them."[23] Their papers were too long. They seemed bent on making history before they studied it. On the first day Hoffer announced that he would personally throw any "punk" who called him a bad name down the nearest flight of stairs. He advised the Berkeley administration to erect a sign: HAVE TEETH: WILL BITE. Having watched from his office window as students burned a car on campus, he threatened to build a giant statue of Clark Kerr so that they would have to look up to him every day on the way to classes. He was disconsolate when Kerr, the "finest product of our educational system," proved finally too weak to defend against "barbarians" the enlightened institution he had helped build.[24]

Despite the anguish his years at Berkeley brought him, Hoffer greatly benefited from the experience. It is probably good that he did not spend his life on a college campus because academic rules and tools might well have spoiled his unique vision; but eight years on one of our best campuses, after he was already a mature thinker, helped broaden his horizons. He came to see that the typical Berkeley student, regardless of age, was essentially a juvenile. "Where there are kids, there are dogs," he once said when asked why Berkeley had such a large canine population.[25] These adolescents, typical of all men gripped by change, were prime prospects for a true believing mass movement, just as the campus movements of the 1960s proved (*EH,* 49). Although they were affluent, or perhaps because they were affluent, they looked like refugees from a depression. Neither children nor adults, they were held in the industrial society's limbo without a primitive culture's rite of passage. By reading these students back into history, Hoffer was able to bring his true believer forward and make him a more contemporary and a more universal figure.[26] The snake, he once said, always pops up in an affluent paradise; and it was no surprise to him that he should appear to modern America at the major universities.[27]

Now, of course, Berkeley is quiet except at football games, its student government is on the conservative side, and its street people are merely quaint. The radicals of the 1960s have turned to Eastern mysticism, to "Jesus," to the establishment; and many of them now warn against the very ideologies they once so loudly advocated. Abbie Hoffman, the radical student leader Hoffer most deeply despised, said in 1978 that he was wrong to have told kids to kill their parents, that he and a bunch of spoiled, selfish brats made the 60's what they were. Hoffer wonders only why it took him and others so long to figure that out.

Early in 1967 appeared *The Temper of Our Time,* a product of the same struggle that had earlier produced *The Ordeal of Change.* Dedicated to Hoffer's academic sponsor Norman Jacobson, *The Temper of Our Time* probed more deeply than *The Ordeal of Change* the traumatic effects of drastic change, which is "the most difficult and dangerous experience" mankind can face. Drastic change, Hoffer said, is the greatest problem of the modern world: the change from backwardness to modernity, from subjection to equality, from poverty to affluence, from work to leisure: it explains the frenzied temper of our time.

The six chapters of *The Temper of Our Time* deal with the personality of the juvenile, the pain and the opportunity that automation-created leisure brings to the masses, the dynamics of the Negro revolution, the quickening pace of "intellectual" control of America, the fallacies of America's naturalist movement, and the character of the post-*Sputnik* age. Hoffer's observations and conclusions, all highly controversial and immensely exciting, demonstrate his white working-class roots. It is a book of deep prejudices, loudly and unashamedly expressed, the best and most honest expression of working class opinion to be published in the 1960s.

S. K. Overbeck, reviewing it for *Newsweek,* called *The Temper of Our Time* a "cool, glittering diamond-hard book—the culmination and refinement of his past works. As such it is a testament to his valuable toughmindedness."[28] Joseph Featherstone, writing for *New Republic,* was much more hostile. He did admit Hoffer's genius for "extending the particulars of his experience into universals, for fashioning moral truths out of his rage for logic." But he lamented Hoffer's willingness to let "good ideas mingle promiscuously with silly ones." Apparently disturbed by Hoffer's harsh indictment of "intellectuals" like himself, he called the book mostly "Sunday Supplement trivia."[29] The professional liberal assault on Hoffer had begun.

In April 1967, Hoffer was forced by time to accept a way of life he had vowed to avoid at all costs. Having completed twenty-five years on the waterfront, he was officially retired. He would receive a $5,200 annual pension from the ILWU, but his working days were supposed to be over. "A pension," he would find, however, "is pay for the work we keep on doing in our dreams after we retire."[30] He would never stop loading and unloading those boats, and many mornings he would rise exhausted from his imaginary nocturnal labors. But now it was time for him to test all his theories about the creative potential of leisure.

The year 1967 also saw Hoffer, after sixteen years of minor literary fame with a select audience, suddenly become something of a pop hero. In 1965 he had done a series of half-hour interviews with educational television station KQED in San Francisco. Aired later on the Public Broadcasting Network, these programs were sufficiently provocative to bring Hoffer's potential as a "star" to the attention of Eric Severeid of CBS News. In the summer of 1967, playing a rather certain hunch, Severeid met Hoffer in a San Francisco hotel room, and with the cameras humming away the two of them talked for several hours. Severeid had the good sense to ask leading questions and let Hoffer recite long, animated passages from his books; and the sixty-minute program constructed from the best exchanges proved an overwhelming success on prime-time commercial television.

Severeid, who admitted that he had once dreaded reading Hoffer because he had heard Eisenhower admired his books, was so certain that the interview was pure gold that he put his own name and prestige on the line. He threatened to cause the network unnamed miseries if they did not show it on prime time in the fall. Reluctantly the network agreed to the odd arrangement, and Hoffer's big, scowling, tortured, laughing longshoreman's face appeared on television screens "coast to coast" on the evening of September 19. The show was titled, perhaps misleadingly but engagingly, "Eric Hoffer: The Passionate State of Mind." The popular response was so massive and so positive that the show was rerun November 10, and the second response surpassed the first.[31]

Kenneth Crawford of *Newsweek* called the show a major news event because Hoffer had had the courage to express "in new ways old ideas whose time had never run out," not even in the skeptical 1960s.[32] Severeid himself explained it this way: "Hoffer had made millions of confused and troubled Americans feel very much better about their country. He had pulled aside the veils of supposed sophistication and, in new ways, showed them again the old truths about America and why they remain alive and valid" (*EH,* xi). Hoffer was seen nationwide as the rare man with the talent to entertain and educate at the same time simply by speaking his mind openly and honestly.

The show brought him fame. He was now able to dine in San Francisco restaurants which had before been off limits to him because he would not wear a necktie. "I'm Eric Hoffer, and this is my town," he loved to say to startled head waiters who were ordered by their managers to seat the man.[33] CBS charted plans (which were never carried out) to have Hoffer do an interview with Severeid once a year. Hoffer's four books began selling at a fast clip. He signed a contract with the Ledger Syndicate to write a column for 214 newspapers. *Time* magazine referred to the upcoming columns as "awesome epigrams" that would, in typical Hoffer fashion, sum up whole civilizations and epochs with epigrammatic flourishes, as they did.[34]

The column, called by some papers "Reflections" and by others simply "Eric Hoffer" and by others both, proved easy for Hoffer to crank out and extremely lucrative. The commission for it plus the jump in his book sales earned him some $180,000 in 1968 alone.[35] Refusing to list deductions, he paid over $70,000 in income taxes that year. He used his earnings to set up an educational trust fund for young Eric (which was never used for that purpose because the boy did not attend college) and to establish the "Eric Hoffer–Lili Fabilli Essay Award" at Berkeley, which would give a $500 annual prize to the best 500-word essay by a Berkeley professor or student. Several persons who wanted to enter the contest inquired about the brevity, suspecting that it was 5,000, not 500, words, but Hoffer was adamant. Any idea, he said, could be stated in 500 words, so he was giving contestants a chance to express two and a half ideas.[36] It was his revenge on wordy Berkeleyites.

The column proved both popular and rewarding (though Hoffer felt he was contributing mostly to the IRS), but after a year he gave it up. "I was spending myself in small change," he says. The man who edited (and profited handsomely by) the column begged Hoffer to continue doing it, but he refused, saying later, "It tickled me to be able to give it up."[37] Lili was especially disturbed by Hoffer's disinclination to profit by his fame, but Hoffer simply told her, "Lili, count your blessings." Tax laws would limit him to "one tiny egg" of a book about every two years, but it was enough. "I've always been spared of greed," he said with satisfaction.

Not all the "rewards" of fame could be so easily refused—or enjoyed. Hoffer's well-publicized televised comments on Lyndon Johnson, by 1967 a much-embattled president conducting a most unpopular war in Southeast Asia, earned Hoffer one job, at first bright with promise, that would burden him the rest of his life. On the Severeid show he had admitted to having no feelings for John Kennedy, "a European" who crossed the Atlantic more often than he crossed the Mississippi. He called Ronald Reagan, then governor of California, a B-picture hero who wanted to turn A-picture California into his kind of low-budget scene. But he called Johnson the "protagonist in the great spiritual drama of the American common man." Warming to his subject as Severeid listened, he said, "I've lived with Johnsons all my life, see, I know them. He'll do the right thing. Let me go all the way—he'll be the foremost President of the twentieth century."[38]

Hoffer had already told *Life* magazine early that year that Johnson "has more humanity in the dirt under one fingernail than all the intellectuals in history."[39] He would tell *Time* magazine early in 1968: "I want to help get Johnson elected. I have known Johnsons all my life. The greatness of this country is that it can produce so many. If he fails, I fail. If he succeeds, I succeed."[40] This was after Johnson, in response to the Severeid show statements, had brought Hoffer to the White House for a personal conference. The two had hit it off from the start. Hoffer said afterward that he had wooed Johnson the way he would have wooed a beautiful woman; and when he talked of how wonderful it was that a "common man" like LBJ could be elected president, Johnson wholeheartedly agreed.

Many people were surprised at Hoffer's Johnsonianism. Liberals could not understand his blindness to the criminal nature of the Vietnam war; and conservatives were aghast that he would so unashamedly support the advocate of civil socialism. The affinity was doubtless as simple as Hoffer said it was. He saw Johnson above all as a common man; and while a common man could make mistakes, he deserved another common man's support. Hoffer has often said that America's greatness lies in her ability to prosper without a ruling elite. "You can close your eyes, reach over to the sidewalk, make a man President—and he'll turn out to be a Truman." No other country in the world is like it. "It's breathtaking."[41] He judges every political leader by one standard: whether he could be elected to office on the waterfront. "We came in with Lincoln," he once told me. "Before him, America wasn't America. It was run by a bunch of aristocratic snobs."

A fairly consistent if somewhat disinterested Democrat until 1968, Hoffer changed his political orientation in the late 1960s. He blamed the Democrats (not LBJ, however) for the mistakes that helped create "that terrible decade" known as the 1960s.[42] He could not bring himself to support Humphrey in 1968, and he found McGovern in 1972 "a pretentious yokel" who would not have been elected president of his local.[43] In *Before the Sabbath* he even suggested that the 1960s might have been avoided had JFK and LBJ been more like Eisenhower than like "the mama's boy" Roosevelt.[44] Nixon he called a tragic figure: "a man of unsurpassed courage" for bombing North Vietnam just before his trip to Moscow but a man ashamed of his commonness, a man of "outstanding intelligence but without mission."[45] Jimmy Carter was virtually a dirty word to Hoffer.

But in 1967–68 he was a Johnson man, and their friendship led to one of Hoffer's most bitter experiences. In response to the summer riots of 1967, Johnson had appointed the "National Advisory Commission on Civil Disorders." Known more commonly as the Kerner Commission after its chairman, the governor of Illinois, this commission was heavily liberal; and its conclusions, drawn together by Mayor John Lindsay of New York City, highly critical of administration policy, angered LBJ. In response to the assassinations of Martin Luther King, Jr. and Robert Kennedy in the spring and early summer of 1968, Johnson appointed the "Commission on the Causes and Prevention of Violence." This time, according to liberal critics like Arthur Schlesinger, Jr., and subcommittee member Jerome Skolnick, the roster was loaded with Johnsonian "conservatives." Milton Eisenhower was chairman. Committee members were Hale Boggs, Philip A. Hart, Roman Hruska, Albert Jenner, A. Leon Higginbotham, Patricia Harris, Leon Jaworski, Terrence Cardinal Cooke, William McCulloch, Ernest W. McFarland, W. Wal-

ter Menninger, and Eric Hoffer. Hoffer, Skolnick would snipe, was
there to represent the American workers' backlash opinions.

The commission was given twelve months (10 June 1968 to 10
June 1969) to complete its task. Richard Nixon, on 23 May 1969,
would extend its life until 10 December 1969. There were sixty
days of hearings by the committee as a whole, during September,
October, and December 1968. Hoffer paid his own expenses to
attend. From beginning to end he was everyone's chief antagonist.
He judged Milton Eisenhower a decent man but one voluntarily
submissive to the liberal, eastern, intellectual, academic establishment; and he was blunt enough to say so. His opinions came more
and more to be regarded as offensively reactionary and were less and
less appreciated. Arthur Schlesinger, Jr., who had once praised *The
True Believer* for its honest portrayal of fascism, now came to see
Hoffer not so much as "one of us without the pedigree" but as a
poorly educated working man full of working men's prejudices.
Among the committee's heavy concentration of conservatives, he
would write in *The Crisis of Confidence,* was "Eric Hoffer, who had
explained away the murder of Senator Kennedy by saying that it
had been done by a foreigner. Had Sirhan Sirhan, who spent half
his life in the United States, won the Nobel Prize," Schlesinger
sniffed, "Mr. Hoffer would no doubt have claimed him as a model
of the American way of life."[46]

It is true that Hoffer was a thorn in the side of his fellow committee
members as well as most of the witnesses, but it is also true that
the reporting subcommittees and their witnesses were heavily liberal-
to-radical in attitude and quite often sought to use the hearings as
a soapbox for the expression of views incompatible with those of an
overwhelming majority of Americans. One report from a University
of California task force—the Skolnick report, published as *The
Politics of Protest*—prompted a disclaimer from Milton Eisenhower
that it did not necessarily represent the conclusions of the commission. This report, like many of the others, did represent current
liberal academic opinion, and it provoked Hoffer to excessive verbal
reaction.

At one point Herman Blake, a black sociologist from the University of California at Santa Cruz, played a two-hour taped interview

with Huey Newton, Black Panther and convicted murderer. Hoffer's angry response ("I did not come three thousand miles to listen to this crap")[47] led to a most irrational and unfortunate exchange. A black witness said, "We are full of rage," and Hoffer shouted back, "Mister, it is easy to be full of rage. It is not so easy to go to work and *build* something." He told the committee that he had lived half his life in poverty and had never asked for a handout. Whereupon black Federal Judge Leon Higginbotham of Philadelphia accused Hoffer of blatant racism: "I think Mr. Hoffer's statements are indicative of the great racist pathology in our country."[48]

Hoffer was accused of being an exemplary witness for the depth of racism in the nation. Televised clips from the hearings caught Hoffer shouting at a bearded Negro in a dashiki. Photographs of his speeches always showed him with his eyes closed, his mouth open, his fist clenched. He was made the butt of jokes and the "bad guy" of the hearings. He was no longer the liberals' friendly sheep dog, their happy accident from the working class; he was now their prototypical bigot, the living example of what was wrong with America, the morning star of Bunkerism. While Hoffer obviously was huffily emotional in stating his "unenlightened" opinions and was driven to irascible excess by the severity of his opposition, we may well imagine how he felt at being exposed to the intolerance of "the tolerant." Americans love dramas with recognizable stock characters. Hoffer permitted himself to be cast in the role of bigot, and then he proceeded to give an award performance.

Hoffer's experience in Washington confirmed all his prejudices about "intellectuals." He developed a particular distaste for sociologists, whom he called the most intellectual of intellectuals, whom he now blames for helping foster the crimes of the 1960s. "Sociologists have a vested interest in turmoil," he came to believe.[49] Far from being the impartial, objective diagnosticians they claim to be, they spend their time calling for change without warning of its harmful and dangerous side effects. During the 1960s, Hoffer contends, they wanted not so much to help the poor as to radicalize them against the established structure of American society.[50] Reacting wildly to the theories of the sociologists he heard during the hearings, Hoffer exclaimed: "Poverty causes crime! That is what they are always shoving down our throats, the misbegotton bastards! Poverty does not cause crime. If it did we would have been buried in crime for most of our history."[51]

Milton Eisenhower, in the letter that accompanied the commission's report, published later as *To Establish Justice, to Insure Domestic Tranquility,* wrote to Richard Nixon: "With one or two notable exceptions, our findings and recommendations have been unanimously agreed to by the thirteen members of this Commission." Hoffer was, of course, the most notable of the exceptions. He was totally opposed to the conclusion that to increase welfare and raise the living standard of blacks and other minorities would automatically eliminate violent crime. The photographs of commission members published with the report show Hoffer, tieless of course, wearing a work cap, the only one not smiling, the only one looking away from the camera. This was unfortunately very apt. From this point his public image would decline, and he would react with ever more biting condemnation of the liberal establishment. He would come to call his prejudices the "testicles of my mind."[52] Whereas he had once written that "vehemence is the expression of a blind effort to support and uphold something that can never stand on its own" and "we are least open to precise knowledge concerning the things we are most vehement about,"[53] he would now begin to taunt the "open minded" intellectuals by saying, "The more you know about a subject, the more reactionary you are going to be about it."[54]

He would never completely escape, or try to escape, really, his racist image. The year 1969 seemed ready to end on a happy note with the publication of his fifth book, *Working and Thinking on the Waterfront.* Although it was a journal written ten years before, it was his first book published after the Severeid interview, and it was being considered as a major book club's alternate selection. He was asked by his publishers, as added insurance of success, to remove several negative references to black work partners and to add a note of admiration for Martin Luther King, Jr. Hoffer's reaction was to tell the book club to "go jump."[55] The book appeared uncut, racism and all, and it was immediately attacked for its bigotry. It is a most honest book, however, and perhaps the best example of how Hoffer's mind works. He picks up an idea from a book or magazine, from a personal experience or observation. He nurses it along from a journal entry to an aphorism to an essay to a book. This is the essential Hoffer at work.

The 1970s: The Creative State of Mind

In 1970 Bill Moyers, in the middle of a continental tour to "listen" to America, found himself at a meeting of the San Francisco Art Commission. An elderly member of the commission, a rough workingman very set in his ways, complained so bitterly about the presence of television cameras in the meeting that eventually he worked himself up into a rage and stormed out. Members who remained behind argued whether he was a spoiled child or a man of great integrity who simply would not tolerate a serious discussion being turned into a circus. The man of course was Eric Hoffer.[56]

Hoffer perhaps found his eighth decade as mixed as the committee's reaction to him. The 1970s were for him a time of increased literary production and receding powers, a time when fame and advancing age combined to make him both happier and sadder than at any other period of his life, a time when his "family" brought him the greatest joy and the most severe pain a man can know. He sometimes—but only sometimes—says, "To the old, the new is usually bad news."[57]

Hoffer thoroughly enjoys being a "somebody" in San Francisco. He takes long walks, makes an occasional public address, serves as "unofficial, self-appointed building inspector" for the city, and basks in the glory of his reputation. "Fame," he once told Stacy Cole, "means you are known by people you don't know. Fame has turned San Francisco into my neighborhood."[58] He might have included most of America in this neighborhood. Still blessed with an absence of greed, he now can say, "I need little to be contented. Two meals a day, tobacco, books that hold my interest, and a little writing each day. This is to me a full life."[59] Long before, he had foretold the end of his days: "The best part of the art of living is to know how to grow old gracefully."[60]

He does miss the physical exertion and comradeship of the waterfront. Once in 1971 he returned to the docks, to help load and publicize the shipment of thirty cartons of his books to Israel; but for the most part he has stayed away, content to watch from his high-rise apartment as the younger generation of workers "labor-fake" their way through the days, something his generation of course never did. He lives near the bay, near the good restaurants, near the heart of the city that he has made his own.

He has continued, even in old age, to have recurring nightmares. They have changed only slightly. Once he dreamed he had no arms (a fear, he says, that he would be punished for not being a writer), and now he dreams he has been sentenced to death for some obscure and half-forgotten crime. This dream, he believes, is his punishment for having "betrayed" his beloved Martha Bauer. He never wrote to her, he never even thought of her for twenty years, and now he thinks of her constantly.

He has for some time thought of himself as a very old man, and this is especially so now that he has almost doubled his expected forty years. "Old age is not a rumor," he says.[61] He speaks often of the misanthropy of the old, their loss of sensuality, which separates them from the human race, as if he fully understands it from personal experience. In his darker moments he says that if he believed in God he would go ahead and kill himself. His celebrated gloom oozes out in statements like, "It's a good thing that I'm dying. Everything now is so depressing."[62] But such moments are relatively rare. He has Lili to watch over him, to give him both her company and his solitude, whichever he needs at the moment. She has obviously prolonged his life and made it much richer than it would have been without her. He refers to her home as the happiest place on earth to him.[63] It makes him say, ruefully, that a man by himself is in bad company.

Yet even his "family" has not been an unmixed blessing. Young Eric has been an almost constant source of anguish, from his bouts with youthful temptations to his final estrangement. From the beginning Hoffer pressed his love and favors on the boy, perhaps too vigorously, and expected more of him than he could or would deliver. The boy reacted with a poor record in school, with an obstinate refusal to be a good "grandson" to Hoffer, and finally by leaving home to make a new life elsewhere. Hoffer is too close to the situation to see that as the boy shuns college, rejects a comfortable home, and heads off to make a life in the wilderness he is imitating his "grandfather" as only the most sincere of flatterers could do.

The 1970s saw the appearance of more new Hoffer books than any other decade. The four of them, "one tiny egg every two years," began with *First Things, Last Things* in 1971. Composed of nine essays, it might well be the best book to begin a study of Hoffer. His major concerns here are the origin of man and man's culture (especially as it relates to cities) and the great effects change is having on America (especially as it brings to power Hoffer's favorite hated antagonist, the intellectual). It is a stimulating and provocative book, and it is not surprising to find that the reviews of this first Hoffer book since his reputation took such a beating in the Violence Commission hearings should be so mixed.

John Seelye, reviewing it for *New Republic,* warned readers not to be too upset with "our resident peasant philosopher" for the excesses of this book. Hoffer, he said, is a typical Californian with the typical "San Andreas Syndrome," which has left him convinced that he lives on the edge of a cataclysmic apocalypse. He is sure that the 1960s were a tumble backward into barbarism, that Visigoths have overrun civilization, and that things are sure to get worse. Seelye found it easy to dismiss Hoffer's "articulate ignorance" and even his condemnation of the "intellectuals" who make up the biggest part of his readership, because he saw Hoffer's bearlike lunges against a frayed leash as just so much playful kidding around; but he did warn that a lot of pedants might be offended by the steady, unending ridicule of their kind.[64] One such pedant was Ronald Berman, Nixon's elitist director of the National Endowment for the Humanities, who wrote in *National Review:* "This book is shot through with some of the most appalling amateurisms in archeology, history, philosophy, and social thought that it has ever been my pleasure to grade C minus."[65] Since Hoffer had never received a teacher's grade in his life, he was not offended by the remark.

After 1972, when Hoffer reached seventy and was retired from the Berkeley classes, he seemed to turn his attention from the city as the origin of man to the vital subject of the modern city's survival. His reaction to the increase of crime in the streets was a militant

call for counteraction. Civilized man's future, like his past, lay in
the city, he said; and if he is to survive he must, like David, take
up a weapon to defend himself against the barbarous giant of chaos.
In June 1973, he addressed seven hundred mayors at their national
conference at the local St. Francis Hotel. He had them on their feet
cheering throughout his speech as he told them that the increase
in crime is due to the meekness of good citizens. "Get mad, Americans!" he shouted. America's future would be decided in the streets
of the cities.[66] The victimized majority must stand up and kick the
violent minority in the teeth. He urged the mayors to make courage
fashionable and to pin medals on people who beat up muggers.[67]
For his part Hoffer purposely continued to walk in dangerous places
alone at night. "They won't bother me," he said. "They can smell
courage. I would grab a mugger by the throat and take him with
me."

In 1973 Hoffer's seventh book, *Reflections on the Human Condition,*
dedicated "to Lili," gave some readers reason to believe Hoffer was
in a state of decline. "Liberal" criticism, represented by Norris
Merchant in *Nation,* accused Hoffer of substituting vacuous naiveté
for patriotism. He even went so far as to compare the aging, "fascist"
Hoffer with his old antagonist Hitler: both of them despised the
"semitic" tradition of prophecy, iconoclasm, and revolution.[68] All
of which is not only frightfully unfair to Hoffer but also demonstrates
a woeful ignorance of his previous work and of this book.

Reflections on the Human Condition is not a great or a particularly
satisfying book. It is made up of 183 aphorisms grouped under five
topical headings: Between the Dragon and the Devil; Troublemakers; Creators; Prognosticators; and The Individual. The aphorisms,
many of them quite memorable, generally, but not necessarily, fit
the topics. The overall impression, despite a few notable exceptions,
is that Hoffer's great writing is past. Yet more direct and indirect
quotations from *Reflections on the Human Condition* have been used
to write this study of Hoffer's thought than have come from any
other of his books. Here can be found Hoffer's best description of
the nature of man and the process of his climb to mastery of the
natural world. Here is Hoffer's most complete and stimulating state-

ment on the creative mind. By 1973 Hoffer may have been unfashionable, but he was not at the end of his road.

By 1976, with *In Our Time,* he seemed to be. This book, dedicated to "Steven and Eric who have taught me much," is a collection of thirty-two essays as brief as those Berkeley faculty members must submit to the Hoffer-Fabilli Contest. Hoffer is still alert and learning here. He still tackles the tough questions. He talks of the potentials of youth and the aged, the contributions the capitalist middle class has made to man's freedom, the constant struggle between man and nature. Yet something is missing, and it may be the true Hoffer spirit. William Gavin believed this was the case. He lamented Hoffer's attempt here to be a nice, optimistic, advisory grandfather. He was saddened to find the man who had survived being admired by those who did not understand him lapsing into such predictable banalities.[69] John F. Mariani, writing for *Saturday Review,* called *In Our Time* a book of Jiminy Cricketisms: vague essays on vague topics that took the declarative sentence to a new low of emptiness.[70]

Hoffer himself, who had long feared that Harper and Row would continue to publish his books even when they turned to "crap," knew that this eighth book was a small accomplishment. He admitted that he had pulled out several of the more biting essays because he no longer cared to bark. He would write in the opening lines of his ninth book, *Before the Sabbath,* that as he finished *In Our Times* he had the distressing feeling that he was "scraping the bottom of the barrel." Yet as Reed Whittemore wrote in the *New York Times,* Hoffer still managed to convey, even here, that wonderful theme of his: that we should all continue to be "learning" rather than "learned" people.[71]

In May 1977 Hoffer suffered a heart attack. It was serious, but it slowed him only briefly. Later in 1977 he did a major interview for Public Broadcasting called "Eric Hoffer: the Crowded Life." Jeanne Wolfe of Miami's WPBT asked the questions, and editor Arla Saare wisely saw to it that she was left out of the final production in favor of long Hoffer narratives. The show, aired on several different evenings early in 1978, was an enormous success. It won a number of prizes, including the Chicago Film Festival's "Best Locally Produced Documentary" and the Valley Forge Freedom Foundation

Award for 1978. Hoffer's appeal was undiminished by time and changing circumstances. He was still an American original.

In the middle and late 1970s, Hoffer found himself, perhaps for the first time since his early years on the bum, being seduced by the kindness of a wealthy man. This time it was Charles Kittrell of the Oklahoma-based Philips Petroleum Company. Mr. Kittrell, a longtime fan of Hoffer, brought him to Bartlesville, treated him to every luxury, made tapes of his talks, and persuaded Hoffer that Anglo-Saxon Soonerland was what made America great. Hoffer was even tempted to eliminate certain criticisms of the rich from his ninth book, but his editors insisted that he not do so, and Hoffer agreed after all that they were best left in. But he did dedicate that ninth book, *Before the Sabbath,* "to Charlie Kittrell with much affection" and argued in private that it was he doing the seducing. He would make the Kittrells of the world Medici.

During the crucial year 1974, after he had "scraped bottom" with *In Our Time,* Hoffer began a diary—a sluice box, he called it—to "wring a few drops of essence from a shrunken mind" the way he had once panned for gold in the panned out mountains near Nevada City. Published in 1979 as *Before the Sabbath,* it proved that Hoffer's mind was not shrunken at all and that his last drops of wine were neither gritty dregs nor diluted residue but a still heady brew. Although the heart of the journal, Hoffer's dealings with young Eric, is missing, the book is vintage Hoffer and stands up well even without its most powerful theme. There are four or five well-stated questions that demand book-length answers; and though the book is full of Hofferian overstatement, repetition, and prejudice, it requires no apology.

William F. Buckley, reviewing it for the *New York Times Book Review,* found in it Hoffer's great, undiminished gift of being able, in grand style, to oppose all a priori thinking.[72] Robert Kirsch, reviewing it for the *Los Angeles Times,* found Hoffer actually learning a new style in his old age. He found this book more relaxed, more reflective, more sure of itself than Hoffer's previous offerings. Whereas the earlier books had won Hoffer admiration and respect, he said, this one would win him affection.[73] Perhaps *Sabbath* proved what Hoffer had long suspected: "The path to uniqueness is to be yourself—but this takes a lifetime."[74]

Life and Work: Philosopher of the Misfits

So Hoffer enters his last years, forever young, forever learning. "Life broke most of the bones in my body," he says, "but it did not run over me" (*EH,* 1).

Hoffer has established himself as modern society's most authentic spokesman for the members of all societies who do not fit into prearranged, neat, safe categories. He understands, he knows these people, because he is one of them. He can see with the eye of an initiate their potential threats and benefits to society. They are the tramps, the pioneers, the weak and rejected who keep moving mankind forward. Hoffer's account of them and the worlds they have created, his evaluation of their role in the past and future, the Hoffer writings grow with each year more valuable to students of the strange animal called man.

This is not to say that Hoffer pretends to offer any final solutions regarding man and his society. His valedictory may well be summed up in his words: "In human affairs every solution serves only to sharpen the problem, to show us more clearly what we are up against. There are no final solutions" (*EH,* 27). It would be a violation of the Hoffer spirit for him or for us to think that his definitive pronouncements are to be taken as gospel. He has always practiced and encouraged his readers to practice the virtues of the inquisitive case.

Chapter Three
The Winemaker

In *Before the Sabbath,* Eric Hoffer, himself both a thinker and an artist, wrote: "The thinker looks for a universal truth that will help explain unique events while the artist endows the unique with an intimation of the universal. What they have in common is that to both the visible is mysterious" (p. 86). Thomas Aquinas once wrote that the philosopher and the poet are "both concerned with the marvelous," and it is this concern that brings Hoffer's two gifts together.

Hoffer is one of those rare persons who can claim both a philosophic and a creative gift, one of the few individuals able both to create and to reflect analytically on the origins and dynamics of his creativity. With his natural sense of the color, the sound, the feel of life, he could have been a painter, a composer, a novelist. Instead, perhaps because of a critical intelligence that drove him well beyond those fields, he became a philosopher who would spend most of his energies studying, analyzing, defining the creative person and the creative act. Yet he remained also an artist, and his analytical writings are themselves works of art.

Creativity

Hoffer believes that man's creative power lies in the "flawed" human character, which renders man the only animal that does not grow old and serious, the only one that carries childhood into adulthood, that continues all his life to laugh and play.[1] "Man is the only young thing in the world," he has said. "The cry of pain and of fear man has in common with other living things; but he alone can smile and laugh" (*EH, #*2). This perpetual childishness, which will be examined more closely in Chapter 5, is for Hoffer man's most unique characteristic, for when man "ceases to be a child, he ceases to be a man."[2] It is "the source of his uniqueness and creativity."[3]

The idea that necessity is the mother of invention is to Hoffer worse than a cliche. It is patently false.[4] Man's first activity was play, and his inventions were all first toys and only later converted to utilitarian instruments. "Man," he says, "was shaped less by what he had to do than by what he did in playful moments." The ascent of man was "enacted in something like an Eden playground rather than on a desolate battlefield." It was certainly no grim affair, for "as we trace back the aptitudes, skills, and practices which enabled man to survive and gain mastery over his environment, we always reach the realm of play" (*EH,* all above quotations from #13). Creative periods of time are and always have been times of frivolity, for "men never philosophize or tinker more freely than when they know that their speculation or tinkering leads to no weighty results."[5] Play, Hoffer concludes, is man's most useful occupation.

The first and foremost by-product of man's play, Hoffer contends, is not invention but art. "Man learned to paint, carve, sculpt, and mold in clay," he says, "long before he made a pot or wove cloth or domesticated an animal. Man as artist is infinitely more ancient than man as a worker" (*EH,* #13). Man the artist is true man, for he is man the eternal child. Hoffer is fond of quoting Baudelaire to the effect that "genius is the recapturing of childhood," and he finds that true artists all have certain childlike traits: (1) total concentration and absorption in their work; (2) a deep and lasting curiosity; (3) a love of play.[6]

This he believes helps explain why the artistic avant-garde is often a gang of childlike undesirables. Like children they are clumsy, inept, undependable in many ways; but they are therefore free and open to new vistas, always in search of fields where no one is expert, where new work is expected to be ill-shaped and forgiven if it is.[7] Like so many of Hoffer's former partners in the fields and on the waterfront, they are both tramps and pioneers. Like children, they gaily tinker, with little sense of grave responsibility or self-consciousness; and their tinkering opens new paths of artistic pursuit for others.[8]

This childlike creative individual is most likely to emerge, according to Hoffer, in the city. Hoffer's "city" is any community of men descended from those earliest of human cities made up of individuals who were originally nomadic hunters but were forced out of communal migratory families by natural disasters: human debris swept along until for mutual protection they gathered behind stockade walls to conquer the iron law of nature. "The city," in contrast to the agricultural "village," accepts as it has always accepted new people and their new ideas and makes them its own. The village, tied to nature's cycles, tied to recurrence rather than to progress, rejects new people and new ideas and is therefore the enemy of creativity.[9] As Hoffer puts it, "Whoever heard of anything new coming out of a village?"[10]

But "the city" (the early one, the modern one) offers the human psyche exactly the comradeship and style of life needed for the development of art. Having studied the Altamira Cave drawings of Spain, Hoffer concluded that "the artistic impulse is likely to emerge where there are leisure, a fascination with objects, and a delight in tinkering and playing with things,"[11] all characteristic of "city" life. Only in cities, free from continual toil, with populations always being renewed from without, societies large and varied enough to demand and afford specialization, can the creative impulse be nurtured to fruition.

Creativity, Hoffer holds, is everywhere, and there is no shortage. All it needs to emerge and bloom is the right atmospheric conditions. The "average" man, Hoffer's "common" man, is fairly "lumpy" with talent. Only elitists, who consider the masses pigs, who are themselves devoid of talent, think talent is rare. Hoffer delights in reminding such "intellectuals" that when a he-pig beds down a she-pig they can produce a Leonardo. Talent is not rare, but we do not yet know how to tap it. "Where the development of talent is concerned we are still in the food-gathering stage," he says. "We don't know how to grow it."[12] We still depend on happy accidents. By studying history, however, we can see certain conditions that encourage its growth, conditions found in certain cities.

For example, Hoffer writes, we know that the golden ages of fifth-century B.C. Athens and Renaissance Florence came when artists did not consider themselves elite and when entire cities encouraged and participated in the arts.[13] The creative milieu of such cities included (1) a measure of individual autonomy; (2) a sense of economic well-being; (3) the absence of destructive mass fervor; (4) little opportunity to waste creative talent on political or social busy work; (5) substantial rewards for meritorious work; (6) and a degree of communal discipline.[14] Even a moderate amount of domestic oppression, if not too harsh, can encourage creativity; for a work of art can be a successful protest against discipline.[15] Studies of the great Catholic artists of the High Renaissance and Baroque periods tend to confirm Hoffer's conjecture.

But Hoffer would add that creativity, no matter how common, no matter how cultivated by proper conditions, comes only from brief flashes of insight and must be captured and energetically molded into works of art. "That which is unique and worthwhile in us makes itself felt only in flashes," Hoffer has written. "If we do not know how to catch and savor these flashes, we are without growth and without exhilaration."[16] Moments of insight, inspiration, revelation come unexpectedly, always, of course, to the prepared mind, and they are brief. If they are not immediately captured, they are lost; and to transform them, nurse them into works of art requires long, hard work. "How much easier is self-sacrifice than self-realization!" Hoffer has mused.[17] At the core of talent, he believes, is the "confidence that by persistence and patience something worthwhile will be realized. Thus talent is a species of vigor."[18]

The persistence that transforms a flash of inspiration into a work of literary or visual art requires mental muscles. "One does not have to be bright," he once told a student who asked how one solves a philosophical problem. "He just has to hang on until the solution presents itself."[19] For Hoffer a "true talent will make do with any technique,"[20] for "style is each man's way of saying the same thing."[21] What makes an artist succeed is his ability to drive a flash of insight to a finished state. "We are told that talent creates its own opportunities," he says, "but it sometimes seems that intense desire creates not only its own opportunities, but its own talents." Furthermore, "by adequate canalization and under favorable circumstances, any kind of enthusiasm, however crude in nature and origin, can be directed into creativeness."[22]

Flashes of inspiration and the energy to pursue them to completion, Hoffer believes, come to and from souls whose strings are stretched tightly by the pull of conflicting desires. Art is the music of taut strings. Creativity is discontent translated into art. "Man's thoughts and imaginings are the music drawn from the taut strings of the soul," he has said. "The stretching of the soul that produces music is the result of a pull of opposites—opposite bents, attachments, yearnings." Where there is no polarity, as Hoffer says is the case with fully accepted orthodox religions, where all energies flow smoothly and in the same direction, "there can be hustle and noise but no music."[23] This accounts for the tendency of creative men to be personally unhappy and the tendency of men who want to be creative but find their gift too meager or beginning to decline to turn destructive. According to Hoffer, we will find no great artists or committed revolutionaries among happily married men.[24] Only men whose souls have been made taut by the pull of opposite desires can make beautiful music or lead fanatic armies. Creativity and destructiveness walk hand in hand, and natural endowment decides which will achieve supremacy in each individual.

In private conversation more than in print, Hoffer's terminology is explicitly sexual. The condition of the soul in the process of creative endeavor, he says, is much like the condition of the male genitalia in the state of sexual excitement. The agitation, the discomfort, and the labor to liberate seminal fluids are the same. He once described his state while writing the "Things Which Are Not" section of *The True Believer*, the most "poetic" section of the book, as "full and fluid."[25] In describing his condition as he wrestled with one philosophic problem, as he moved nearer a solution, he said he "had a mental hard-on." For Hoffer, desire is the raw material of creativity, and the creative individual is as passionate in his pursuit of truth and/or beauty as the lover is of his beloved.[26]

Passion in and of itself is of course not sufficient to produce art. The very passion that drives the artist to complete his creative work drives the untalented person to pursue destructive adventures in mass movements. The truly creative person, Hoffer says, can be said to work without obvious emotion, for sound and fury proceed from the soul without the tools to complete a task. It is talent that separates the artist from the fanatic, the creative person from the destructive person. Talent alone enables one to see significance in things common and commonplace, the source of all great art. "Only the creative mind sees as much significance in the common as in the great," Hoffer says; for the creative act, he believes, is the process of taking things from the cesspool and making them beautiful. "It is the mark of the creator that he makes something out of nothing."[27] All experiences of all men may be "equidistant from a truth or regularity," but it is only the creatively talented mind that finds a common occurrence as significant as an outstanding event—and only such a person who can create a truly outstanding work of art.[28] While "in all ages men have fought most desperately for beautiful cities yet to be built and gardens yet to be planted,"[29] it is only the artist who can see such cities and gardens in common human property and can build and cultivate with the skill and determination required for lasting achievement. Creative talent is the ability to "introduce order into the randomness of nature."[30]

The creative person, artist and writer, not only sees things that others cannot see and brings to fulfillment dreams others cannot nurture to maturity; he also makes himself superfluous. Like the great teacher whose students can learn without him, the artist "creates something that has a life of its own, something that can exist and function without him."[31] This accounts for the widespread anonymity of much artistic expression. Hoffer contends that entire styles in the arts are quite often triggered by unknown, unremembered artists who found joy in creative release but never found fame. Noticing that in a certain California town all the lawns were lush and cut to perfection, Hoffer followed one of his frequent "hunches" and visited the town's cemetery. He found that the earliest settlers in the area had come from the part of England best known for its wonderful lawns. The early artists who inspire fashions and style are often unremembered, yet they continue to exercise power over worlds they never dreamed would be.[32] "Many who have shaped history," Hoffer concludes with the sentiment of an Oliver Goldsmith, " are buried in unmarked and unvisited graves."[33]

The urge to create can be a great blessing—to the individual, to the world—but it can also be a curse to both. It is accompanied by multiple dangers, the most important of which is that the other side of creativity is destructive fanaticism. According to Hoffer, "the source of man's creativeness is in his deficiencies; he creates to compensate himself for what he lacks."[34] The unfinished animal called man became *homo faber,* a maker of tools and weapons, to compensate for his lack of specialized organs needed to survive on earth. Man became *homo ludens,* man the playful and thus man the inventor, because he lacked the genetic compulsion to grow old and serious. He learned to speak because his lack of instinct and telepathy demanded oral communication. So long as his deficiencies do not include talent, he can fulfill himself through his quest for compensation. Should his creative flow prove weak or prematurely finite, he may be ripe for conversion to a fanatic cause and its mass movement.[35]

Just as "the thwarted impulse toward action" and its inner tensions result in creativity, so, too, can it lead to passionate involvement in the kind of mass movement Hoffer has spent so much time studying and considers almost always destructive to the fabric of man's society. "People thus thwarted tend to become either revolutionaries or writers, artists, etc., depending on a person's natural endowments."[36] The man with talent creates; the man without talent shakes the world. Thus, according to Hoffer, "those who seek but fail to obtain power become creators (if they have the talent), and those who seek to create but cannot gravitate to power (if they can) as True Believers."[37]

The passion to create, if thwarted, takes possession of a person. While the truly creative person creates with a minimum of sound and fury, the "passionate state of mind" is usually a substitute for confidence, indicating a lack of skills, talent, or power.[38] As Hoffer likes to put it, "Where there is the necessary skill to move mountains, there is no need for the faith that moves mountains."[39] The faith that motivates the true believer is born of the frustrated passion to create. A mass movement gives the untalented person, who prefers alibis to opportunities,[40] a chance to be part of a society of resentment,[41] a society that excuses failure and sublimates frustrated urges into frenzied activities that demand total, mindless commitment. "People who cannot grow want to leap," he explains; "they want shortcuts to fame, fortune, and happiness."[42] The revolutionary never grows up because he cannot grow, while the creative person never grows up because he never stops growing (*EH, #*12).

Another danger that lies in the pathway of the truly talented person is that he is constantly tempted to consider himself more than a laborer, as someone unique and therefore weighty, as the center of the universe, the bearer of a destiny "shaped by cosmic forces."[43] "Where thought is prompted by a penchant for weightiness and a high purpose," Hoffer says, "the result is often a blend of pompousness and hysteria."[44] There is a great temptation to feel just such a sense of importance, to dramatize oneself, to act a part, and to feel terribly angry and alienated.[45]

Although he has himself elevated creativity to the highest levels of human achievement and often says he gladly bows at the altar of creativity, Hoffer would have writers and artists remember that they are simply craftsmen, laborers. If they regularly remind themselves that the greatest of Renaissance artists referred to themselves as *lavoratore,* maybe they can avoid the common folly of self-dramatization and pathetic alienation and excusatory mass movements. For in the final analysis, "the compulsion to take ourselves seriously is in inverse proportion to our creative capacity."[46] Utopia for Hoffer, if he did not consider utopia as one of the true believer's most dangerous dreams, might be a society in which the writer of books and the binder of books are equal social partners.[47]

Hoffer's own greatest fear, apparently since early adulthood, has been not so much that he might become a frustrated fanatic but that he might just fritter away his talent, waste his time on busy work, and fail to fulfill his promise.[48] He believes that quite a number of writers, including the great John Milton during his "active" years in Puritan politics, did waste time and energy on lesser work; and he has assiduously avoided doing so himself. "Wasting ourselves is sometimes a way of camouflaging our worthlessness," he wrote in *The Passionate State of Mind.* "We hereby maintain the fiction that there was aught worth wasting."[49] In Hoffer's case there was little cause to worry. Full of "seminal" ideas, he was continually tumescent, as bound to write as to talk or make love and in much the same style: precisely, explosively, like the beloved Beethoven symphonies of his youth.

Writing has never been easy for Hoffer. It has always been a matter of adding "crumb to crumb." Talent in his case is indeed a species of vigor. "Since the publishing of a couple of books," he once wrote, "I have been cast in the role of a writer and, without being aware of the utter absurdity of it, I have come to expect things to flow out of my fingertips. The truth is that I have to hammer out each sentence, and must hang on to an idea for ages if aught worthwhile is to be written."[50] But he once listed "a little writing each day" as one of his few vital needs; and he still knows of nothing more beautiful than a good sentence; and he believes that a few of his good sentences will survive him because they will continue to catch in people's minds and germinate.[51] To fashion a few more of those "few good sentences," he works on and on.

Hoffer seems to understand better than most "professional" writers the danger of words. "Words have ruined more souls than any devil's agency," he once wrote. "It is strange that the word, which is a chief ingredient of human uniqueness, should also be a chief instrument of dehumanization."[52] Hoffer's first title for the despised "intellectual" was "man of words," and he has always considered the man of words and his words among the greatest of threats to man's well-being. Behind every destructive mass movement was a word to inspire it. "When you have split everything and reduced it to its smallest component, you will find a word," Hoffer says. "That word started it all."[53] It was of course the intellectual who spoke that word.

"The typical writer," Hoffer once complained, "will judge a society by how it honors men of words."[54] The first writers, he believes, were scribes, men trained to perform a practical task. "Writing was invented not to write books but to keep books." Only when the scribes lost their jobs due to an excess of personnel or the disintegration of an empire did they become writers, filling pages with the songs of their own personal woe, borrowing style from illiterate bards. Amos of Palestine, Homer of Hellas—the examples abound.[55] Such writers produced great literary traditions; but they also used their words, especially if their songs failed to find appreciative recognition, to stir the masses against the established social and political orders. They have on occasion led mass action against states.[56]

The modern "intellectual," the untalented, unappreciated, frustrated man of words, has always been one of Hoffer's chief concerns. "One of the chief problems a modern society has to face," he has said, "is how to provide an outlet for the intellectual's restless energies yet deny him power. How to make and keep him a paper tiger" (*EH,* 21). More, much more of this will follow.

The Teachers

Hoffer the writer did not, as we have seen, emerge early or quickly. He spent more than thirty years mastering his craft, training himself to use his powers of observation and expression effectively, before his first book was published. He learned from people he met along the migratory trails and on the waterfront and from the writers whose books were his constant companions during his long, solitary intellectual pilgrimage. These writers were his teachers. "There are no chaste minds," he has written. Minds copulate whenever they meet."[57]

The first five of his teachers, as I have described his listing them for me, are French with a fairly strong Jewish flavor: Montaigne, Pascal, de Tocqueville, Renan, and Bergson. The second five are Bacon, Wells, Dostoevski, Burckhardt, and the Hebrew Bible. The subject matter he would pursue for a lifetime—the nature of man, his society, his government, his religion—came from de Tocqueville, Bergson, Burckhardt, and to a lesser degree from Bacon, Wells, and Renan. His style of writing, the essay, the aphorism, came from Montaigne, Pascal, Renan, and Bacon. From Dostoevski he borrowed a concrete and realistic but cosmically dramatic approach to life and art. In the Bible, as in Renan, he found both the illuminating story of that unique species of *homo sapiens,* the Jews, and a poetic literary beauty unexcelled in world literature.

Hoffer does not read French, but it is the language of his favorite authors. He loves the way French writers state their clearly defined statements in simple forms. Writers from his parents' native Germany he finds too wordy and obtuse for his taste. The idea that to be profound something must be dark, difficult, and abstruse he believes is a German superstition. The really great "German" writers were not, he says, German at all. Heine was a Jew, Burckhardt was Swiss, and Nietzsche claimed to be a Pole.[58] Hoffer rejects all artificial erudition, all suffocating verbiage, all German superstition, and works for French clarity of thought and simplicity of expression.

A good example of his attitude toward writers who violate such rules of writing is his reaction to the Greek philosopher Plato. Hoffer claims he cannot understand Plato. He believes Plato (an intellectual) completely misrepresented Socrates, who was a simple man, a stone mason, the kind of man who would have told stories to illustrate his ideas, not engaged in endless sophisticated dialogue with straw men. Socrates, Hoffer believes, would have been far more human than Plato's Socrates. All of which is probably true—and demonstrates that Hoffer has understood Plato and Socrates far better than most professors of philosophy. Plato and his descendants everywhere, the intellectuals, make simple truths complex and themselves kings of common men.

It is not hard to find the mature Hoffer in the lives and writings of the teachers he so much admired. Of this most impressive group, Michel Eyqeum de Montaigne (1533–1592) was the most important to Hoffer. It was Montaigne who first inspired Hoffer to write and showed him how to do it. He was the eldest of eight children born to an aristocratic Gascon-French merchant and his Portuguese-born Jewish wife. His father, a mayor of Bordeaux, was granted the privilege of fortifying his home, and to this castle's tower Montaigne would in his middle years retire to write his famous *Essays*. Michel was trained in law. He was introduced to court. But though he was a Catholic and despite his love for "pagan" classical writers, he was known to be friendly to the French Protestant Huguenots; and for many years guilt by association denied him the political position his talents demanded. At thirty-eight he married a woman of wealth and retired to a life of the mind. During the next nine years, until his first book was published when he was forty-seven (only two years younger than Hoffer when his first book was published), he spent his time inventing a new literary genre, the personal essay. His first attempts at the new form, mostly notes on books he read, were piecemeal and without significant value; but as he developed his style, his essays became both more inclusive and more conclusive; and the later ones were both autobiographical and more universal. The best of them were written with a detached subjectivity Hoffer always found entertaining and inspiring, and he patterned his own work after them.

Montaigne was himself Mayor of Bordeaux twice, and upon the ascension of Henry IV Navarre he was offered a high government post, which he had to decline due to declining health. His public career never reached fulfillment, a fact Hoffer would applaud; but his writing gained international renown. He has been, in every age since his death, a favorite of sober doubters, those who love literature rich in reflection and humor, those who know that in the final analysis man can know and understand only himself through his personal experience.

Hoffer first read Montaigne in the old Florio translation. Florio, who translated Montaigne in 1613, has been strongly criticized for liberties he took with the original text, which occasioned what many linguists consider major errors that mislead readers. But for Hoffer, who used Montaigne mainly as a springboard to his own personal reflections on the human condition, such errors are probably insignificant. What he owes to Montaigne, and to the Florio translation in particular, is his style.[59] The Montaigne-Florio sentences have hooks that catch in the mind and germinate. Hoffer has passionately sought to write such sentences himself, and much of his merit as a writer lies in his obvious success.

If Montaigne published his first book almost as late as Hoffer published his, Blaise Pascal (1623–1662) died at about the time Hoffer expected throughout his early life that he would die. Whether Pascal's early death attracted Hoffer to him no one knows, but his style and subject matter certainly did. Pascal, like Hoffer, demonstrated early genius for physics. At the age of eighteen he invented a sophisticated calculator. Also like Hoffer, he found science too narrow and turned ever more to a philosophical study of man. He was known to have friends among the heretical Roman Catholic Jansenists and was accused of holding dangerous personal opinions. His *Pensées*, one of the books that has most influenced Hoffer's style and thought, concluded that while God is for the most part hidden from man's understanding, the search for God and God's will is man's most exciting and rewarding adventure.

Hoffer bears the imprint of Pascal's personality perhaps more than Montaigne's. Pascal's mind, like Hoffer's, was existentially responsive to life. He developed a prose style, as did Hoffer, that succinctly made its point and often shocked his readers into creative response. He used tight logic, forceful imagery, and carefully constructed sentences to convey deep convictions set free to be remolded by receptive minds. Hoffer, one of those receptive minds, is perhaps Pascal's most devoted and successful twentieth-century disciple.

If Montaigne taught Hoffer his style and Pascal taught him his philosophic expression, Alexis de Tocqueville (1805–1859) taught him his political science. Hoffer considers de Tocqueville the greatest of political theorists, and from de Tocqueville he took cues about the nature and destiny of man the political animal. De Tocqueville, born into the French minor nobility, studied law and served for a time as an assistant magistrate, but boredom eventually prodded him to apply for a leave of absence to study penal methods in the young "Jacksonian" United States. At the end of a two-year sojourn in this "Europe transplanted to a wilderness," de Tocqueville returned to France to write the book that would make him immortal: *La Democratie en Amerique* (1835). Imitating Pascal's literary style, using a somewhat naive but penetrating logic, he made the first and some would say still the best analysis of the American federal system. Hoffer has said, only half facetiously, that the greatest thing about de Tocqueville was his courageous willingness to write before he knew anything. He played his hunches and took chances and made major discoveries.

Democracy in America, written by a man who was European and born to the old way of life, evaluated the strange new American system from the vantage point of a foreigner whose own country was involved in a democratic experiment. While he could and did applaud the aim of democracy—to check the centralization of power in the hands of an aristocratic oligarchy—he could not help but see that a complete leveling of the political realm might critically limit a society's resistance to some future proletarian despotism. The very process of eliminating a trained aristocracy might well pave the way for a new and even less flexible and more oppressive totalitarianism of a "democratic" mass movement.

De Tocqueville spent his middle years in active political service as a member of the French Chamber of Deputies. Hoffer considers this a tragedy akin to the years John Milton "wasted" writing tracts for the Puritan cause; but for de Tocqueville it was a much-needed training period, a time to learn from practical experience and primary observation, akin to the time Machiavelli spent serving the Florentine Republic before he was forced into retirement to write *The Prince*. During his years as a representative, de Tocqueville wrote little of lasting value; but when at the end of his service he had the leisure, he wrote perhaps his greatest book, one that reflects the practical knowledge of public affairs he could have learned only from public service: *The Ancient Regime and the Revolution*.

A number of Hoffer's central themes, the political and social questions he pursued throughout his long career, his willingness to play hunches and take chances and speak when he is not sure of himself, may be traced to de Tocqueville's writings. Most important of all, it was de Tocqueville who taught Hoffer to beware of self-proclaimed political saviors who would use slogans like "the brotherhood of man" as stepping stones to dictatorial power.

Ernst Renan (1823–1892), fully as important to Hoffer's development as Montaigne, Pascal, or de Tocqueville, was his professor of religion. A native of Brittany, a lifelong student of linguistics and religious studies, Renan was still another French Catholic whose writings raised ecclesiastical eyebrows and sometimes hackles. His two most famous books, *The Origins of Christianity* and *A History of Israel* (five volumes), describe Christianity and its parent Judaism as natural human phenomena that do not require divine or miraculous defenses or explanations. Another of the marvelous stylists Hoffer admires so much, Renan is also said to have had the most thorough understanding of group psychology and social dynamics of any student of religions before, during, or since his time.

Hoffer says that Renan taught him to understand the human condition. He believes that Renan can tell us more about present-day problems than any contemporary writer.[60] It was Renan who

taught Hoffer to appreciate the Jewish role in world history and
started him on his road to vigorous support of the state of Israel.
It was Renan who taught him to judge every modern nation by the
way it treats its Jews, by the opportunities it offers them, by the
directions within it their energies take them.

Speaking of Jews, the fifth of Hoffer's masters, Henri Bergson
(1859–1941), taught him his sociology and set him off on his search
for the causes and consequences of change. It is in a way surprising
(and puts the lie to Hoffer's claim not to be able to understand
sophisticated philosophy) that Hoffer would have responded favor-
ably to Bergson because many readers have found him as obtuse as
any German. Perhaps Bergson's biography, his bitter experience as
a Jew in a "Christian" world, held Hoffer's attention long enough
for Hoffer to want to pay the considerable price that Bergson demands of his students.

Bergson was born in Paris of Jewish parents. His chief scholastic
interests were philosophical intuition and the dynamics of change.
In *The Two Sources of Morality and Religion* (1932) he sought to prove,
as does Hoffer, that life is free and creative and always producing
something new. Accused of being antiintellectual, as Hoffer often
has been, Bergson argued that all he wanted to do by questioning
academic assumptions and methods was to free scholars of their
strictly delineated disciplines, to free them to pursue truth wherever
it might be found. Offered exemption from incarceration by the
Nazis because of his age and because he was a Nobel laureate (1927),
Bergson earned the honor of martyrdom by dying with fellow Jews
in a prison camp the year after Hitler's army occupied Paris.

British writers have had less influence on Hoffer than the French,
but he does include two in his list of teachers: Bacon and Wells.
Sir Francis Bacon (1561–1626) was the first of these two and heads
Hoffer's second five. A prominent politician and office holder under
King James I, Bacon is known for his political treatise *The New
Atlantis* and for his *Wisdom of the Ancients,* the latter an allegorical
interpretation of the eternal truths hidden in ancient mythologies.
But it was probably his *Essays* (1625) that most influenced Hoffer.
Written in the King James English of the Authorized Bible and of
Florio's Montaigne, Bacon's *Essays* is a collection of brief aphorisms

expanded into fifty-eight essays. Dedicated to the proposition that "the monuments of wit survive the monuments of power," these essays, replete with memorably quotable internal aphorisms, learned illustrations, and brilliant metaphors, are coldly unsentimental analyses of the political, social, and religious problems of his and all ages. They are Hoffer's cup of tea.

Bacon's life, his style of writing, and his subject matter all appealed to the young Hoffer. He would spend his life studying politics in a Baconian manner and capture the essence of his astute observations about man in a Baconian style. He might also ruefully agree with Bacon's oft-quoted aphorism: "He that hath a wife and children hath given hostages to fortune."

The other Englishman on Hoffer's list, H. G. Wells (1866–1946), shared Hoffer's lack of early formal education and his predilection for the sciences. Having educated himself through constant reading while he worked, Wells proved sufficiently self-educated to earn a scholarship to study biology with T. H. Huxley. His books, however, while they demonstrate great scientific sophistication, are concerned with the meaning of history, which is of course one of Hoffer's central themes. Wells wrote two histories of the world, one of which was the famous *Outline of History* (1920), and thirty volumes of political analysis and prophecy, these in addition to his myriad volumes of fiction. One of his books, *First and Last Things,* doubtless inspired the title of Hoffer's *First Things, Last Things.* Wells was the self-made man par excellence, a man the British might call "trans-Atlantic" in his drive and ultimate success, the perfect example of Hoffer's uncommon common man.

Feodor Mikhailovich Dostoevski (1821–1881) has always been Hoffer's favorite novelist. Dostoevski's *The Idiot* was the first book Hoffer read after he recovered his sight at fifteen. A Russian who came to love the Tsar's chains, he seems at first an unlikely choice for Hoffer's list of teachers; but his masterful handling of the sounds and sights of real life has always captivated Hoffer. Perhaps it is Dostoevski's ability to capture the pain of cosmic loneliness that first attracted Hoffer. Perhaps in Dostoevski's long speeches, attributed to his gargantuan antiheroes, Hoffer found the plain truth about the drama of man's existence. Hoffer may himself be seen as a Dostoevskian character, consciously or unconsciously patterning his life after the enormously buoyant, burdened characters caught in this world's ironic vice. Hoffer's very existence, like theirs, is a personification of courage. His philosophy, like theirs, is a labor of courageous love.

Jacob Burckhardt (1818–1897) is Hoffer's only German teacher, and as Hoffer is careful to point out Burckhardt was Swiss. A historian of arts and letters, a polished scholar of the most enlightened "Romantic" tradition, Burckhardt focused his attention on the "great men" of various historical epochs, from *Constantine the Great* to the heroes of *The Renaissance in Italy*. Burckhardt's thesis, as Hoffer saw it and adopted it for his own uses, is that the great men of each era create the social milieu in which all men must live and develop. Men make the age.

Hoffer, who denies that man is a mere tool of circumstance, has never written the history of a particular era; but his studies of early man, his studies of man in great ages, his studies of the kind of men who set the tone and style of each age, tend to verify Burckhardt's thesis. He would disagree with Burckhardt only when he talks of America, for here the "great man" is the common man who can be picked out of any crowd and made leader. Perhaps even Hoffer's one great weakness, his tendency to stereotype people by national and social and even racial character, is a product of his study of Burckhardt, who was Hoffer's professor of history.

The Bible, particularly the Old Testament, which Hoffer has always found so fascinating, was written over a period of five hundred years by scores of writers. The sense of history, the political sophistication, even the theology found in the Hebrew Bible show signs of evolution; yet running like a thread through the complex groupings of books is the Hebrew sense of man's unique character, of the significance of human history, and of this world as a testing ground for man's potential. These assumptions have all found their way into Hoffer's philosophy. Hoffer has remarked about how often he finds references to God in his writings despite the fact that he does not believe in God. He should not be surprised really, considering how inseparable the concept of a personal God is from a Hebraic (and Hofferian) view of life.

So the man who never attended public school has been a student of some of the greatest teachers of all time. Few are as fortunate as Hoffer to have both the freedom and the will to find the excellence of style and thought that sits on every library shelf for anyone who wants to learn.

The Art of Letters

Hoffer the artist and philosopher has never actually set down a plan for achieving literary excellence; but he has left us his example and has scattered through his writings clues to his success, which are also by implication suggestions for other writers. His advice may be listed under fourteen points. The first four are fatherly warnings.

1. First he would say to stay free of binding commitments to people, places, and ideologies. "Man is distinguished from the animals by language and by thought," Hoffer has said, "and both must be free."[61] He has of course been only partially successful in following his own advice. Though he believes there are no happily married creative artists, he has given himself in all but name to marriage and fatherhood. He has tied himself to the city of San Francisco and even to certain rooms that he has left with great reluctance. He has committed himself to a secular faith in the American common man and the system under which he works; and this has at times rather strictly limited his vision and caused him great pain. But for years, as he discovered his themes and wrote his most seminal passages, he was indeed free; and even the restrictions of his later commitments have not robbed him of the benefits of this early freedom.

2. He would also warn the aspiring writer to avoid the company of "literary" people. He recognizes that the growing mind needs community, and that "minds copulate whenever they meet";[62] but hobnobbing with "professional" writers, he says, is worse than a waste of time. "There is not a single great writer or artist I . . . would want as a friend, companion or neighbor," he has written. "Envy, vanity, malice and sheer rudeness seem to be characteristic elements of the creative personality."[63] The aspiring writer, Hoffer has concluded at the end of forty years of writing, should "be left alone to stew in his own juice."[64] The results of such stewing will

be far superior to the results of hopping from one literary party to another.

3. Hoffer would also say to stay free of partisan political causes and their time-consuming busy work. Hoffer was himself a nominal Democrat until the late 1960s, but except for his endorsement of Lyndon Johnson he has never involved himself in party politics. He has never offered himself as a candidate for union or public office and seldom ever took an active part in elections unless some close personal friend happened to be running. Milton, Machiavelli, and de Tocqueville all prove to him that the period of a writer's life devoted to politics is apt to be sterile. The writer may learn a few things from such experiences, but Hoffer believes the main lesson will always be that he has wasted his time.

4. Hoffer would say to stay free also of professionalism. The writer should earn his bread by common labor and write in his spare time. He should choose the "dullest" of work, compose as he works, write when he has finished. Above all, he should avoid the sterilization of being labeled and of coming to think of himself as a "professional" writer. For Hoffer the waterfront was the perfect creative milieu. He has often chided "intellectuals" who consider "dull" work inhuman. Among his most exciting and rewarding days were those spent unloading cargo, trading light talk with a partner, and composing beautiful sentences with "the other side" of his mind. "The outstanding characteristic of man's creativeness," he said, "is the ability to transmute trivial impulses into momentous consequences."[65] From a newspaper article, from a chance conversation with an illiterate worker, from a fleeting visual image on the dock, have come some of Hoffer's most profound conclusions. Language, he believes, was invented to release energy. "Perhaps the first human words were part of a work chant."[66] So what better place is there to chew on a fascinating problem until it is transmuted into a literary solution than while doing dull work.

5. On a more positive side, once the writer has avoided these four traps, then he must allow himself to fall in love with ideas. Ideas, Hoffer says, are not ponderous; they are light; they dance. "I love ideas as much as I love women," he has said. "I derive a sensual pleasure from playing with ideas. Genuine ideas dance and sing.

They sparkle and twinkle with mirth and mischief. They titillate the mind, kindle the imagination, and warm the heart."[67] Furthermore, "If they do not dance like ballerinas, they are no good."[68] They must be set free, and the writer must learn to savor their simple yet complex beauty and respond creatively to their delights.[69] Even in his old age Hoffer still jumps with joy at the approach of a dancing idea. He gives it all his attention; he applies all of his seductive charms to its capture; and once it is his he gives it free rein to take him on the grandest of adventures.

6. Once a ballerina-idea has captured a writer's fancy, once he has made it his guide, then Hoffer would advise him to find other ideas to dance beside it and form a ballet. To find other ideas, some its equal, others merely supporting dancers, he should depend on chance acquaintance, remembering of course that as Pasteur said, "Chance favors the prepared mind." "Expose yourself to chance," Hoffer says; for the prepared mind will be lucky.[70]

Hoffer once described allegorically and most humorously how he finds his ideas. Suppose a man comes to San Francisco to meet a friend but has no idea where his friend lives. How does he find him? "My way," Hoffer said, "is to stand on the corner of Powell and Market and wait for him to come by. And if you have all the time in the world and you are interested in the passing scene, this is as good a way as any; and if you don't meet him, you are going to meet someone else" (*EH*, 22). This method has been working for Hoffer's "lucky" mind for half a century. He has met some very interesting people and ideas.

7. But suppose a ballerina the writer discovers and wants for his own belongs to someone else? Hoffer's advice is to steal her away. He loves to quote T. S. Eliot: "Immature poets imitate—mature poets steal." To imitate, he says, is to turn wine into water—to steal and translate what is stolen into something quite new is to turn water into wine. This is always a risky business because "the real anti-Christ is he who turns the wine of an original idea into the water of mediocrity"; but the risk is worthwhile because to "swallow other people's ideas, digest them, produce something new" is the greatest challenge of life.[71]

Originality, as Hoffer defines it, is what we do with what we did not originate; and the ability to assimilate creatively the work of someone else is the ability to grow. The Greeks took the Phoenician alphabet and created a literature the Phoenicians never dreamed of.[72] The cow eats grass and turns grass into milk. Hoffer advises those who want to see the process of appropriation and assimilation in progress to go back and find what his "authorities" actually said and compare the original statements with his own paraphrases of them. He stole. He made what he stole his own. He retrained his ballerinas to dance to his own music.

8. After assembling his ballerinas and finding their potentials, the writer should carefully and slowly mold them into his ballet. He should let them build up the pressure of his soul. He should stew in his own creative juices until his provocative dancers carry him to a creative burst of energy. From his state of sensual excitement, from his agitation, from the ejaculatory burst of thought will come the scenario and movements to form his ballet of truth.

9. The "prepared mind" that can recognize prima ballerinas in the common crowd, that can see his production to its final hard-earned performance, is above all a mind of great stamina. "At the core of every true talent," Hoffer says, "there is an awareness of the difficulties inherent in any achievement, and the confidence that by persistence and patience something worthwhile will be realized. Thus, talent is a species of vigor" (*EH,* 24). Hoffer defines thinking as the mind's muscles hanging on to a problem. "One does not have to be very bright—all he has to do is hang on until the solution presents itself."[73] The writer must read, take detailed notes on what he reads, organize and rearrange ideas, labor long and hard for the right words, and not stop until he is finished. "One cannot read without writing," he says, "or write without reading. One learns to write by reading the efforts of other writers and rearranging, reexpressing the thoughts in one's own words."[74] The finished product of such effort may appear to be commonplace statements immediately recognized as true; but this is simply a sign of the hard work that covers its own tracks. The philosopher shows the reader what he already knows but does not know that he knows. It is a

demanding profession. Hoffer, by his own confession, has found writing difficult.

10. The music for the ballet, the words themselves, must be composed orally. Great writing, Hoffer believes, is always spoken before it is written. Hoffer's books were all recited orally many times before they were committed to paper; and, as has been pointed out, he sent the only copy of each of his books through the United States mail without fear of its being lost because he could have rewritten each one verbatim. He has said that he cares little for grammar or parts of speech, all of which merely confuse a writer. He says he wants simply to hear the music of words. Sören Kierkegaard must have felt much the same way about writing, for he once wrote: "I could sometimes sit for hours, in love with the sound of speech . . . like a flute player entertaining himself with the flute. What I have written was most of it many times, perhaps a dozen times spoken aloud before it was written down."[75] For Hoffer, "there are few things so subtle and beautiful as a good sentence."[76]

11. The ballet and its music, the final production, should be clear and simple in design and line, profound yet easy to follow and understand. "Our conceptions of things are usually more complex than the things themselves," Hoffer warns. "The tendency to complicate things is part of the process of trying to camouflage the emptiness of life."[77] He warns against weighty words that seek to give "deeper reasons" for things, for deeper always means less worthy reasons. To look too closely at a problem is to miss its real significance and probably its solution. This is certainly true of man, he says, for man is all surface, all skin, like an onion, without a core.[78] Just as wine tasters take only a sip of each wine to discover its true body, so should the writer observe and describe only the surface of things.

12. The best way to achieve clarity in surface reality is to use as few words as possible. "I have never had absolute command of language," Hoffer says. "Words have always been to me accidental, unnatural, uninevitable. I have spent my life trying to master words, but they never became part of me. I always have to search for them, pull them in by the neck. I use as few of them as I can."[79] Hoffer's books, against the advice of editors and the expectations of reviewers,

have remained consistently brief and directly to the point. Verbosity, he says, is a sign of ignorance. Long ago he discovered that when he found two books by the same author, one long and one short, the short book was always the first written. In it the author told all he knew; in the longer, later book he tried to hide or make excuses for all he did not know.[80] "We always use more words than are necessary when we try to say more than we know," he concludes.[81]

13. It is wise to be brief, and it is wise to repeat. "If history can repeat itself," Hoffer huffs, "why can't I?"[82] He repeats himself often and without apology. "Of course, every repetition is a little different—like a screw that repeats itself but each time goes a little deeper."[83] Repetition in written discourse, if used wisely, is as aesthetically pleasing as it is in ballet; and it can provide an aid to clarity of theme that no other device can give.

14. Be brief, repeat, and exaggerate. Exaggeration in writing, as on the stage, is the barb that hooks in the mind. Hoffer likes to quote Bagehot, "To illustrate a principle, you must exaggerate much, and you must omit much," and he believes that one should exaggerate even at the expense of accuracy. "It is impossible to think clearly in understatements. Thought is a process of exaggeration. The refusal to exaggerate is not infrequently an alibi for the disinclination to think or praise."[84] Hoffer has gone so far as to say, "Lying is creative; telling the truth is mere reporting."[85] Such statements might call Hoffer's whole body of writing into question were he some grand authority dispensing absolute truth. His self-confessed distortions drive us to see him for what he really is: an enormously gifted provocateur, a planter of seed for future thought and discovery, and most of all a questioner. "Language was invented to ask questions," he says. "Answers may be given by grunts and gestures, but questions must be spoken. Humanness came of age when man asked the first question."[86] Thus Eric Hoffer, the inquisitive case.

Chapter Four
The Wine

Eric Hoffer has followed his sensuous, dancing ideas through nine books over thirty years of writing. These books, filled with their subtle and beautiful sentences, are the fruit of a lifetime of thought and work; and they deserve attention in and of themselves.

The True Believer (1951)

The True Believer was Hoffer's first and some say still his best book. To date it has sold 50,000 copies in hardback and 350,000 in paperback editions and has long since taken its place as one of the classics of American social commentary. It is not a perfect book. In places its organization is a bit didactic. Some of the "authoritative" quotations and paraphrases, which Hoffer included to make New York editors take him seriously, fail to make exactly the point Hoffer wants them to make. Like all of Hoffer's books, it both benefits and suffers from its author's disciplined brevity. It is rife with stereotypes of humankind. Despite a modest disclaimer and scattered modifying statements, it sees all revolutionary movements as basically destructive and their leaders (and followers) as men deeply frustrated by an irredeemably blemished selfhood. Nevertheless, *The True Believer* is a book of profound social and psychological insight, and it rightfully stands in its place as one of the most significant books written by an American in the twentieth century. It studies the figure that Hoffer saw everywhere on the march, shaping the world in his own image.

Hoffer first raises and answers the question: "What Makes Mass Movements Appealing?" He gives three answers. First is the desire for change. Men who are dissatisfied with themselves tend to locate the forces that shape their existence, the causes of their discontent, outside themselves and to feel that if they change the world around them they will cure their own malaise. Extreme destitution can of course thwart action. The desperately dissatisfied person needs also a sense of hope and faith in the future—plus a profound ignorance of the difficulties to be faced. "It is as if ivied maidens and garlanded youths were to herald the four horsemen of the apocalypse," Hoffer says in describing the naive beginnings and tragic ends of most mass movements. To plunge headlong into a mass movement, men must be

. . . intensely discontented yet not destitute, and they must have the feeling that by the possession of some potent doctrine, infallible leader or some new technique they have access to a source of irresistible power. They must also have an extravagant conception of the prospects and potentialities of the future. Finally, they must be wholly ignorant of the difficulties involved in the vast undertaking. Experience is a handicap. (11)[1]

A second reason mass movements are attractive to so many people is a widespread longing among men of discontent for substitutes. A mass movement offers men a new identity, a new self for an old, despised one. It offers, in familiar contemporary terms, a new birth. A mass movement has lost its momentum, Hoffer notes, when it ceases to call men to lay down their old selves and find a new self by identifying with a new cause, when it begins handing out offices and attracting men more interested in careers than in changing the world. A mass movement, to remain vital, must teach its followers to hate today as much as they hate their old selves and to be ready to die if necessary to bring about a new, unspoiled tomorrow.

The third reason they attract followers is that mass movements are essentially interchangeable. A certain kind of person will be a true believer and search for a cause to serve; and which cause it is, so long as it offers him a new identity, is not really so important. One mass movement can be stopped only by substituting another mass movement for it; and such a substitution is not at all difficult to accomplish. Followers of the first will gladly switch over to the second. Hoffer believes that the key to American political stability is that the ever newly arriving immigrants, as ripe for revolution as their cousins in Europe, were given new names, a new language, and new opportunities in a new land where they could build new lives. One mass movement, one with positive direction, replaced one that might have been terribly destructive.

A second question, perhaps more fascinating even than the first, is: Who are the "potential converts" to a mass movement? Hoffer's general answer, before going on to list and discuss each subgroup separately, is that they are the volatile minorities on the fringes of society. They are never the inert, satisfied middle classes. Converts are always people searching for escape from spoiled lives, searching for a cause that will give their lives meaning, people willing to sacrifice the present for the future, the here and now for the there and then. More specifically, they are (1) the poor, (2) the misfits, (3) the inordinately selfish, (4) the ambitious, (5) minorities, (6) the bored, and (7) sinners.

Hoffer spends more time on "the poor" than on any other group. Perhaps having lived an early life of poverty, he understood these people better than the others. The poor most likely to become true believers, he says, are not the abject, chronically burdened poor but the newly poor, those who remember and long for better days. "Where people toil from sunrise to sunset for a bare living, they nurse no grievances and dream no dreams," he says (27). It is those who are close to affluence, either in time or in space, who nurse hatreds and dream of new worlds; for "the intensity of discontent seems to be in inverse proportion to the distance from the object fervently desired" (28).

New poverty is no worse, however, than new freedom among the poor. The gift of freedom is often a curse because it suddenly makes the freedman responsible for his actions and even for his poverty. He craves fraternity, company for his misery, and he may join a mass movement to be free of his freedom. Being part of a close-knit family or social unit, even if the family or unit is quite poor, prevents true believing; but when freedom comes to the poor man due to the disintegration of his traditional corporate society, he may flee his miserable, responsible isolation and join a dramatic cause.

The only poor man who is free of the frustration required to create a true believer, Hoffer says, is the creative poor. As long as a man can be creative, he has self-worth; and self-worth mitigates against true believing. Only if a man's creativity begins to dry up is he a potential convert. Hoffer believes that most fanatics are both sexually and creatively impotent men who live in societies that value both kinds of potency highly. The mass movement is for them sublimatory compensation.

Misfits, Hoffer's second category of potential converts, come in two types. There are temporary misfits—adolescents, the unemployed, veterans, and newly arrived immigrants—who are not irredeemably estranged from society and are generally not ripe for conversion. It is the permanent misfits, those with lasting mental or physical defects, the chronically adolescent and unemployed and estranged, especially those with unfulfilled dreams of creativity, who become true believers.

The inordinately selfish, Hoffer says, actually hate themselves. They join causes that require selflessness. Their pendula seem to swing full distance, from extreme selfishness to extreme selflessness; yet the extreme emphasis on self, whether selfish or selfless, is much the same regardless of the direction of the swing.

The ambitious are prime candidates for conversion because they already deprecate the present in favor of the future, a major requirement for entry into a mass movement. They prefer a society of undefined and supposedly infinite goals to the safety of a stable corporate society with fixed, limited potentials.

Members of minorities, so long as they remain secure in the structure of the minority society, are not generally candidates for conversion. It is only when one of them leaves the social shelter and seeks assimilation into the larger society that he is tempted to join a mass movement. Oddly enough, the least and most successful breakaways are the most frustrated and ripest for conversion. The least successful must live with rejection, while the most successful come to feel superior to the majority.

Boredom comes from a conscious alienation from a corporate society. Only isolated individuals can be bored because they alone can be frustrated. A cause, any cause, fills their empty lives with activity and therefore with hope. It stills for a time the most terrible of fears, the fear of meaninglessness.

Finally, there are the sinners, people with a deep sense of guilt for past misdeeds. A mass movement offers the sinner a new life, a chance to be free of the old guilty self, and an opportunity to perform the same misdeeds for a "legitimate" cause. Hoffer does not but might well add that a mass movement offers an opportunity to compensate for sins.

The third section of *The True Believer* deals with factors which promote the self sacrifice needed to originate a mass movement and agents that promote the unity of purpose necessary to perpetuate it. Hoffer says at the beginning of this section that he expects to be heartily criticized for some of the things he will say but that since this is not a textbook he will not hesitate to proclaim half truths if they hint at new approaches or help to formulate new questions. This section, the least inhibited by Hoffer's fear of academic criticism, is perhaps the most creative and original in the book.

Factors promoting self-sacrifice are (1) the ability to identify with a secure collective whole; (2) the satisfaction of playing make-believe ("Glory is largely a theatrical concept" [67]); (3) a desire to deprecate the present in favor of a proffered future; (4) dreams of "things which are not"; (5) dogma, even when it is irrational, which sets up a "fact-proof screen between the faithful and the realities of the world," (78); (6) and the passion that grows out of the frustration of being estranged from one's own self. Armies, Hoffer says, use all of these factors to create selfless esprit de corps; but an army cannot claim totalitarian control over its members the way a mass movement can because an army deals with the possible while for the selfless legions of a mass movement nothing is impossible.

Once the movement's members are selfless, other factors serve to unify them. One factor is hate. True believers need to confront a common evil, strong and foreign, so as to have a common object of hatred.

A second factor is imitation. True believers need common patterns of "good" to imitate as much as they need common patterns of evil to hate. By imitation they free themselves of their old selves and become someone new.

A third factor is coercion. Hoffer says that propaganda never really changes anyone's mind because propaganda is believed only by those who desperately want to believe already. Propaganda merely justifies coercion, and it is coercion that makes converts and holds them in place. The fanaticism of men who have been unified by coercion is in fact their need to cover up their cowardice and inner uncertainty. Proselytization is a sign of desperate need to prove one's faith to oneself.

A fourth factor is strong leadership. The leader of a mass movement is the director of a great program of make-believe. He need not be particularly intelligent, imaginative, or moral. All he needs to be successful is audacity, fanatic faith, awareness of the importance of the collective mind, and the gift of evoking passion in followers.

A fifth factor is action. Action strips men of concern for themselves. It keeps them too busy to think for themselves. "Teamwork," Hoffer says, "is rare in the intellectual or artistic undertaking, but common and almost indispensable among men of action" (118), men involved in mass movements.

A sixth and final factor is spying. Spying keeps people busy, makes them feel they are serving a sacred cause, and promotes conformity because men know that if they are watching others, others are certainly watching them. It also promotes that very necessary feeling of self-contempt, which makes the movement all the more attractive because by sharpening "eyes for the imperfections of others" (121), it sharpens eyes for the imperfections of oneself.

Overall, Hoffer says, unification removes the frustration of living with a ruined self and gives the individual a new identity. It does not cure the true believer's insecurity because he must continually see that his lifeline to the collective body is in good repair. He is still incomplete when alone. He has indeed traded, and gladly, one slavery for another.

In the fourth and final section of the book, entitled "Beginning and End," Hoffer discusses the three kinds of men who start, lead, and consolidate the mass movement. They are, using his designations, "men of words," "fanatics," and "men of practical affairs."

Men of words (later to be called intellectuals) alone can start a mass movement, for they alone can undermine social and political institutions by familiarizing the masses with the need for and possibilities of change. They destroy security and create a hunger for the "faith" that promises to move mountains. Men of words may vary in style, but they are all literate, they all crave recognition, and they all prefer the appearance of power to power itself. They can be tamed by deferential gestures. They usually end their careers tragically and terribly disillusioned. Only a few, but a significant few, become men of action.

Men of action, the fanatics of a mass movement, lead the revolutionary phase of the movement. Such men are often uncreative and therefore frustrated men of words. The chaos created by men of words is the perfect element for the fanatic. In it he feels he can destroy the old and bring in the new world where he will no longer be a failure. The time of the fanatic's leadership, the time of true believers, is really quite short. He must soon be purged if the movement is to consolidate its gains and settle into permanent leadership. But during his time, the time Hoffer considers sterile, he is indispensable. His self-righteous, petty, rude personality is just what the active phase needs.

When the active phase is over, the movement either destroys itself or is moderated into a more or less permanent institution. In the latter case, spontaneity turns to habit, faith becomes duty, and cause is translated into career. The true believer is either purged or moderated so much that he is unrecognizable. The man of practical affairs takes over. As Hoffer succinctly puts it, "A movement is pioneered by men of words, materialized by fanatics and consolidated by men of action" (146).

At the end of his analysis, as if to correct an impression he knew he was making, Hoffer avers that mass movements can be useful, can bring positive results. They can overthrow incompetent governments and invigorate societies. But "however different the holy causes people die for," he still believes, "they perhaps die basically for the same thing" (xiii).

The Passionate State of Mind (1955)

Hoffer's second book, from which the Severeid CBS interview took its name, is a collection of 280 aphorisms. His justification for publishing a book in this form, other than the obvious fact that to have converted these aphorisms into a more fluently organized book would have taken another year or more, is perhaps found in aphorism 161: "It will perhaps never be possible to speak about our inner life in precise scientific terms. The choice is between poetry and aphorism. The latter is probably the less vague" (91).[2] These aphorisms, gleaned from the notebooks Hoffer kept during the 1930s and 1940s, reflect a brilliantly perceptive mind, one vitally interested in man and man's world; yet aphorisms alone, without organization and unity, do not satisfy a reader's hunger for clearly stated theses.

In one sense *The Passionate State of Mind* is not a book. Its 280 parts are only loosely organized around certain vague themes. It has little focus. Perhaps Hoffer hurried it to print to take advantage of the great critical success that still accompanied *The True Believer*. Perhaps he hoped the uneven repetition would "tighten the screws" with each additional turn. At any rate, the aphorisms, each one a passionate statement on man's passion, can be usefully read as a collection of meditations, one at a time, perhaps one a day, to be examined at leisure. An example is number 219: "Man staggers through life yapped at by his reason, pulled and shoved by his appetites, whispered to by fears, beckoned by hopes. Small wonder that what he craves most is self-forgetting" (121). Here indeed are seed for long and deep contemplation.

The book is loosely organized, in a somewhat crazy-quilt fashion, around four major themes. The first of these themes is the self. "The short-lived self, teetering on the edge of irrevocable extinction" (35), is the source of man's actions because it is the source of man's fears, Hoffer believes. We know ourselves only by hear-say, he says, and "are what other people say we are" (75). We play the roles in which other people cast us, imitating the reflections of ourselves in their eyes (130). We gladly deceive ourselves, lying loudest when we lie to ourselves, and we happily believe our own rhetoric (154). Only the few who do come to know themselves can ever develop the much needed self-esteem that prevents being attracted to some self-forgetting mass movement; the great majority of men, without self-esteem, look for pride in some movement outside themselves and can easily be made true believers (35). *The Passionate State of Mind* is not anthropologically optimistic.

There is also much in this book about one of Hoffer's favorite groups, the weak. The weak, he says, often conquer the strong because their very insecurity drives them to unite and turn their weakness into strength (35). They are particularly gifted in turning guilt to self-righteousness, lack of confidence into faith, and self-hate into group pride. They have a talent for persuading themselves that they suffer for something when in reality they suffer from something, "that they are showing the way when they are running away" from a hated self (36). They have all the qualities needed to fuel a mass movement. In times of great change, when the talents and skills of the strong are of no real advantage, the weak may well lead the world, for in those times tramps become pioneers. They can make the world much better than it was—or much worse.

Hoffer also explores in *The Passionate State of Mind* a theme he would return to examine in almost every subsequent book, the threats of self-appointed social reformers. In order to make his prophecies of doom or utopia come true, Hoffer says, the reformer must gain the power necessary to shape the future; and to shape the future he must both rearrange the past and manipulate the present. The great threat to society in his surges for power is that the self-proclaimed reformer actually hates the world of man. He especially hates it if it lets him change it. He is perfectly willing to sacrifice people to his plans for the improvement of mankind. His programs are almost always fatal. "Those who proclaim the brotherhood of man," Hoffer says, "fight every war as if it were a civil war" (115). The men who "would sacrifice a generation to realize an ideal are the enemies of mankind" (83).

Behind all of his talk of the self, the weak, and reformers, however, Hoffer's real subject is passion. The book is well named, for its central concern is the man who shakes the world because he is driven by a passionate mind, the kind of man Hoffer has named the true believer. Passion, Hoffer believes, derives from an inner dissatisfaction with one's self, a dissatisfaction so deep and distressing that one shrinks from himself and becomes a fugitive (1). "Every intense desire," he explains, "is perhaps basically a desire to be different from what we are" (10).

Such passion, he goes on, is usually found in people suddenly isolated from corporate groups that once gave them meaning. The passionate individual is a person suddenly aware of being alone in society (2). This autonomous person is unbalanced by his individuality and must continually prove himself worthy of the life he feels he does not deserve (27). Inside himself he is the prototypical totalitarian, driving himself from one personally established five-year plan to another (28), always trying to prove that he is not what he knows he is. He can be quite heroic in his vain attempts to escape his failures (52) and in all of his posturing he demonstrates the dramatic skills needed to prove that he is someone other than the isolated self he wishes to escape (56).

"Excessive desire is thus a means of suppressing our sense of worthlessness" (9), Hoffer concludes, for "every extreme attitude is a flight from the self" (10). Such passions almost always take on the tone we traditionally call "religious." There is evident in the passionate person's actions a vivid awareness of weakness and worthlessness, a deep sense of remorse, and a passionate search for a new identity (55). But even dissipation can be a passionate attempt to liquidate an unwanted self, and it should surprise no one that so many saints were once such low sinners, for movements that attract passionate minds are interchangeable (10). All a mass movement need do is give the passionate man the opportunity to believe in a cause and trade in his old, spoiled life for a new one. He gladly becomes a passionate advocate of any cause, for he must persuade others in order to persuade himself (36).

The passionate man, Hoffer believes, was born to spend his life catching up (208). The best motivation for running ahead of the pack is the fear of running behind it. Passion demonstrates a lack of elementary skills. "Where there is the necessary technical skill to move mountains," Hoffer says, "there is no need for the faith that moves mountains" (12). Further, the passionate mind is usually quite uncreative. He longs to be creative, and this longing is the raw material the talented use to create; but the untalented, uncreative man can use his energy only to convulse the world.

Yet Hoffer does offer a ray of hope in an otherwise rather gloomy survey. While man is capable of destructive passion, he is also capable of constructive compassion. Compassion, Hoffer says, is the soul's only antitoxin (139). Where compassion can be found, even man's natural poisons are rendered harmless. Courage, honor, hope, faith, duty, all of these grand characteristics can be twisted by passion into intruments of oppression. Only compassion stands apart as a quality no fanatic can use for the wrong purposes. Compassion, not the principle of justice, guards man from injustice (140).

While the passionate man is unbalanced, isolated, longing to be rid of his independent, hated self, the compassionate man follows the leadership of the "still small voice" heard only in the quiet of inner equilibrium and tries to end his isolation by reaching out to help other men. Hoffer personally believes that compassion is a far more plentiful commodity than most people think. He has found it everywhere throughout his life. The true believer may be everywhere on the march, but the man of compassion abides.

The Passionate State of Mind contains the seed of most of Hoffer's later thought. It will be easy to see these seed spring up and bloom in his later books.

Working and Thinking on the Waterfront (1959, 1969)

In 1958 Hoffer was trying to write a book about "men of words," the much despised "intellectuals," but found himself unable to concentrate. So he decided to "sort things out" by keeping a journal; and between 1 June 1958 and 21 May 1959, he filled seven small notebooks with his day-by-day thoughts. Seven years later he found those notebooks, read them in one long, fascinated sitting, shared them with Lili who suggested he send them to Harper and Row, and saw them published in 1969 as *Working and Thinking on the Waterfront*.

As has been noted, Hoffer told an audience at Boston College that his editors told him while the book was being printed that a major book club wanted to make it an alternate selection but wanted Hoffer to delete several somewhat uncomplimentary references to Negroes, disclaim any racial prejudices, and write a short statement in praise of Martin Luther King, Jr. There were in the manuscript— and there are in the book—disparaging remarks—critical comments, really—about black writer Redding Saunders. There are references to Negroes in Hoffer's ever blacker ILWU, comments about their laziness, their hard drinking, their oversized families. Hoffer also refers to his ever blacker neighborhood, the drinking, the noise, the local prostitution. He says in one place that blacks are in trouble because they believe white prejudices; and he says that blacks need a few real heroes to inspire them because none of their leaders is worthy of imitation (26, 34).[3] Hoffer listened to the suggestions about moderation, but he had just finished his weeks on the violence commission and was in no mood to compromise, so he refused to change a word. *Working and Thinking on the Water-front,* warts and all, served to confirm the racist image he had been gathering about him. Few critics stopped to think that it was ten years old when published.

The book is, despite its underlying racist theme, a veritable treasure trove of Hofferisms. It shows more clearly than any of his other books the way his mind works, how he fluctuates between periods of idle hypochondria and passionate creativity, the way he finds and poses a question, chews on it, keeps coming back to it with other questions, how he adds crumb to crumb until he has an answer and the raw material for an essay. It shows how he pursues each question with amorous determination, how he labors over each thought and each word, each sentence, each paragraph. It shows that he can write only when he is also working on the docks. At one point he comments: "During the whole day I have not spoken half a dozen sentences yet I feel as if I had been engaged in an interminable dialogue. The optimal milieu for me is to be surrounded by people and not be part of them" (51).

It also demonstrates, beyond any doubt, that Hoffer's philosophy is essentially that of the "common" laboring man. On the waterfront he notices that America's uniqueness lies in its working class, in their practical creativity, in their gift for maintenance, in their inate ability to spot phony "intellectuals" who would lead them astray. He suggests, with only minor facetiousness, that longshoremen be our delegates to the United Nations. He relishes telling how his fellow workers helped him write an article for a New York magazine. He glories in being a member of a class of people who need no supervision because America has given them a chance to prove what they can do without supervisors.

The book also reflects Hoffer's deepening relationship with the Osbornes. He takes Lili and the little boy, who is now two years old, to the park and on trips; he buys them presents; he thoroughly enjoys their company. Yet he broods long and deeply over every spat, and he despises Selden Osborne as only a rival can. One entry has him praising Lili as a good mother and the boy as bright and promising. Another has him accusing Selden of being the typical intellectual, a complaining failure, a man incapable of winning the respect he so pathetically covets. Still another has him bemoaning a dreadful dinner with the Osbornes when the boy informed him that he did not "belong to this house" and Selden smiled (60–61). It is obvious that he wants to be with them and suffers in their presence, that he loves them dearly and senses approaching doom.

The book also reflects Hoffer's continuing, growing obsession with the "intellectual," the subject of the book he is trying with little success to write. He speaks constantly of the "man of words" who triggers mass movements, who blasts the roadblocks before him instead of turning them into works of art. The intellectual, he says, actually hates the common men he champions. He is at heart a schoolmaster, and when he takes over a society he "turns it into a vast schoolroom with a population of cowed, captive pupils cringing at his feet" (165–66). He believes that "the vigor and health of a society are determined by the quality of the common people rather than that of the cultural elite" (93).

Finally, the book reflects a dramatic expansion of Hoffer's mind and interests. The 1950s have forced him to examine the emerging third world and apply his social theories to its unfolding drama. He meets a delegation of political leaders and students from southeast Asia, finds them terribly defensive and rude, treats them rudely in turn, and learns a lot from the experience. He advises a consultant from the United States Information Service that the United States cannot give the underdeveloped countries our faith or even our pride. These things they must and will find for themselves. All we can give them are our skills in tackling problems. We should never try to "win over" the intellectuals who run the underdeveloped countries, for they will never stop hating us for our success and commonness.

Working and Thinking on the Waterfront, because it is totally without pretension, without self-consciousness, because it offers such a clear glimpse into Hoffer's working mind, is one of his most valuable books. It shows him working among people, observing them, staying apart to himself, working and thinking, being Eric Hoffer. It can be read with little effort, yet its questions stay with the reader to provoke further thought.

The Ordeal of Change (1963)

Hoffer's third published book, the fourth written, is in many ways his best. It refines the blunt genius of *The True Believer,* surpasses *The Passionate State of Mind* in clarity, and probes more systematically the new problems posed in *Working and Thinking on the Waterfront.* It is composed of sixteen brief essays, taken mostly from Hoffer's personal experiences, which show that with his now well established fame he feels confident to reply on his own observations and judgments rather than looking for "authorities." *The Ordeal of Change* is the work of a man running easily with a second wind.

It provides us with Hoffer's philosophy of history. It demonstrates his ability to grasp the larger dimensions of any subject without having to know its details. Hoffer's history was not learned in academia, and he makes asides that will not stand close scrutiny; but he is also free of restrictions that tend to retard professional historians and render them incapable of giant, imaginative leaps into history's meaning.

The first essay deals with the problems caused by drastic change. A population undergoing drastic change, Hoffer says, will inevitably produce misfits who are passionately ripe for conversion to a mass movement. Change causes revolution as surely as revolution causes change. Man is the victim before he is the agent: "Where self-confidence and self-esteem seem unattainable, the emerging individual becomes a highly explosive entity. He tries to derive a sense of confidence and of worth by embracing some absolute truth and by identifying himself with the spectacular doings of a leader of some collective body" (9).[4]

Essay two looks at the recent awakening of Asia and its conversion to communism. Asia, Hoffer says, is searching for pride. The West brought it change, cracked the old communal framework, and emancipated a race of people to the tragic isolation of individualism. In their isolation, hating the painful freedom forced upon them, Asians by the millions have found pride in a mass movement that let them submerge themselves in collectivization. Europe, he explains, faced a similar situation in the sixteenth century but had a release valve in the form of a new world to conquer. Having no such overseas empire to subdue, Asia must use its energies and find comfort in revolution.

Essay three deals with the "intellectuals" who rule the emerging Third World. Since they are self-appointed saviors who value elitist positions, they naturally hate "common" America. Before the Renaissance, Hoffer says, the man of letters was a "kept" servant who was honored for his skills. Since the spread of literacy has rendered his skills common, he has been an unattached, explosive troublemaker. It is only natural that he would feel at home under a communist regime, where once again he has a respected place and can help direct man's lives.

In essay four Hoffer explains why backward countries resent America so much. They actually want desperately to imitate us, but imitation to them means submission. They must first destroy our credibility before they can imitate us freely. Since imitation demands rigid social unity and conformity, westernization comes quickest in the least western, most dictatorial, most paternalistic states. Since a faith is most easily transmitted by its own heresies, Hoffer argues, communism is a capitalist rather than a Christian heresy, transmitting capitalist programs while claiming to bury the capitalist West. Since only a faith that is very much alive can spawn heresies, Hoffer declares capitalism alive and well.

Essay five asks the question: What is the greatest problem facing Communist regimes around the world? Hoffer's answer is the unwillingness of people in a controlled economic system to work. Westerners think people naturally like to work, but it has been only since the emergence of the unstable, autonomous individual, who feels he must continually prove his worth, justify his existence, that the desire to work has been a potent factor in human affairs. Workers do not love work; they work hard only to kill work. In fifty centuries of human history, only once has autonomous man been given a real chance to prove himself through work, and that is in the American experiment.

Essay six discusses the relationship between the intellectual and the masses. The intellectual's assumed role as champion of the masses, Hoffer believes, is relatively new. Through most of history, with the exception perhaps of the Hebrew prophets, intellectuals have been allied with rulers. Pen rode beside whip in the tallest of saddles. Only in the modern world, without power, aware of the power latent in the masses, has the intellectual pretended sympathy for the common man. Despite the act he displays, however, he is still at heart an aristocrat, and once in power he will always treat the masses as the dirt he really considers them to be.

Essay seven discusses "the practical sense," which Hoffer argues is a recent, perhaps accidental skill, one that emerged as traditional Christianity faded. It developed in the fertile minds of men whose individual freedom drove them to try to prove their worth. Hoffer describes how the practical sense was aided by the way the intellectual and the merchant, the scribe and the trader, cracked each other's monopolies. The scribe made people distrust the trader, while the trader spread the scribe's skill of writing to the common man.

Essay eight, a truly seminal speculation on "Jehovah and the Machine Age," says that the modern western world was able to discover and use science so effectively because of the kind of God it worshiped. Jehovah was seen as a master craftsman, a machine maker, and the early scientists were on a religious quest to find the laws their God had built into his great cosmic machine. Modern science thus had its genesis in the imitation of God. Hoffer could have added, consistently with his earlier comments about imitation, that it was perhaps inevitable that the imitators, to avoid feeling inferior, would in the end discredit the very God they imitated.

Essay nine deals with the workingman and management in the modern industrial society. Hoffer says that it is far better to keep labor and management separate and distinct, amiable adversaries, because societies where the lion and the lamb lie down together inevitably stagnate. Here Hoffer introduces one of his more prominent later ideas: that it is "better to be bossed by men of little faith, who set their hearts on toys, than by men animated by lofty ideals who are ready to sacrifice themselves and others for a cause" (82). He prefers middlebrow bosses to intellectual dictators.

In essay ten Hoffer examines the somewhat surprising upheavals of recent years in absolutist communist countries. They are the result, he believes, of the rise in hope. Distant hope is an opiate, but immediate hope is a stimulant. The countries experiencing upheavals are near enough to wealthy, capitalist western Europe to be inspired to demand a similar combination of prosperity and freedom at home.

Essay eleven, on brotherhood, grew out of Hoffer's conversations with men on the docks. Hoffer concludes, as did his fellow workers, that before a man can love his neighbor he must first love himself. The truth is that we do treat our neighbor as we treat ourselves. To love oneself in a healthy way is prerequisite to loving one's fellow man.

Essay twelve defines individual freedom as the product of a social balance of two dominant forces either one of which operating freely and alone would mean totalitarian rule. Hoffer gives Poland as his chief example. Neither the church nor the state there actually believes in individual freedom; but by limiting each other's power the two of them provide more individual freedom than can be found anywhere else in eastern Europe.

In essay thirteen Hoffer speaks again, and more clearly, of the metamorphoses of the man who through history is first scribe, then writer, then rebel. The early scribe became a writer when the social system that made him crumbled. If he had real literary talent, he went on writing; if not, he turned his pen to the task of stirring up movements aimed at restoring him to his old place of honor, near the throne.

Essay fourteen introduces Hoffer's new theme of the importance of the playful mood. The first machines, he explains, were the toys of young men at play. All of man's greatest inventions, as well as his greatest philosophical insights, came from play. This theme will become more important to Hoffer and his scheme of history in later books.

Essay fifteen contrasts the simple, direct laws of nature with the complexities of human nature and concludes from the disparity that human nature is unnatural. The unnaturalness of human nature, as Hoffer puts it, is due to man's unfinishedness, to the fact that he is an incomplete animal; and his unfinishedness has made him a creator, a maker of artificial organs, to compensate for his natural deficiencies. Man's society, reflecting man's own unfinishedness, his unnaturalness, is inherently disorderly; and only those who hate human nature try to order human society. The "strong" humans are more nearly natural than the "weak" ones, the misfits, who are forced to become pioneers in order to survive a hostile world.

Essay sixteen, the conclusion to Hoffer's grand drama of change, contains Hoffer's often told story of the federal work camp at El Centro where he lived for part of 1934. There he found all of the world's misfits, mental and physical defectives of every type, all incapable of living in a settled society, all of them tramps. There Hoffer came to see that all pioneers are at heart tramps forced out of corporate societies onto the frontiers of human experience. This is one of Hoffer's best essays, and it demonstrates clearly how he is able to find whole worlds of meaning in each grain of sand.

The Ordeal of Change will never be as well known or as widely read as *The True Believer*. It is in many ways, however, Hoffer's best book. It is a book for pioneers, for readers who are not afraid to approach the frontiers of human thought. It is a book of liberation.

The Temper of Our Time (1967)

Hoffer's fourth book is a collection of six magazine articles done over the ten-year period before 1967. In previous books he had written for himself and had spent his energies answering his own questions. In *The Temper of Our Time,* now that he is a "responsible" public figure, he is writing for editors and answering their questions. Yet this is still a rich book—rich in method and in content—and it demonstrates Hoffer's gift for taking every question two or three steps beyond ordinary speculation. It is also about change and its consequences, for as Hoffer opens his comments: "We are discovering that broken habits can be more painful and crippling than broken bones, and that disintegrating values may have as deadly a fallout as disintegrating atoms" (ix–x).[5]

Essay one, "A Time of Juveniles," discusses the interesting fact that through most of history, just as in the 1960s, the world has been shaped by young people. Juvenility, which can emerge at any age in a person's life, is caused by drastic change that forces a person out of one way of life but does not give him another. There is, Hoffer says, a "family likeness" among adolescents, migrants, religious converts, and retirees: they share a confusing, distressing in-betweenness. They are all misfits. Their passion to prove themselves, to prove they deserve to exist, creates a "madhouse" within a social system. Change scoops people up, makes juveniles of them, and encourages them to join packs.

Essay two goes into the dangers and promises of modern technological automation, which is freeing man to pursue a life of leisure. Hoffer says that the new machinery at first frightened him because he feared the social consequences of taking away from thousands of skilled laborers their only way of proving their worth: "There is nothing more explosive than a skilled population condemned to inaction" (24). But as he reflected more on the problem he began to see that the inevitable explosion need not be destructive, that it could just as well release a creative flow of energy and produce a renaissance. One way to make sure this happens, he says, is to turn the whole of society into a school where everyone can learn what he wants to know, learn at his own pace, never stop learning, and reach his full potential.

During the years of concern over automation, Hoffer accepted a number of opportunities to lecture; and in his lectures he devised and adapted a myth to explain modern man's place in the history of work. He told audiences that Adam's vow to return to Eden is about to be fulfilled. The first machines used man the way an iron bull made for the delight of the King of Phalaris used men to make its anguished roars, Hoffer said, but the later machines have brought man back to the gates of Eden: "We stand there panting, caked with sweat and dust, afraid to realize that the seventh day of the second creation is here and the ultimate sabbath is spread out before us" (46).

Essay three addresses, for the first time in Hoffer's printed thought, the Negro revolution. Hoffer says that the Negro's main problem is not lack of opportunity but lack of pride. The Negro actually believes white opinion of him. Hoffer suggests that he start being his own author, that he cast himself in the role of hero, that he return to the South and carve out a successful "homeland" the way the Jews have done in Palestine. He says that Negro leaders have failed to provide such opportunities because they are basically intellectuals and have little faith in the Negro masses.

The Negro's problems, Hoffer admits, have no easy solutions. He cannot emigrate to a new country and take a new name and learn a new language the way European immigrants to this country did a hundred years ago. He cannot escape this country in the North or West. He is still black. Even the Black Muslims, who do offer a type of new birth, will not long be able to avoid the inevitable commercialism of the Americanization process. The Negro's only hope, as Hoffer sees it, is that middle-class black leaders will return to the ghetto and help lead a building campaign that will give the Negro a new sense of pride.

Essay four searches for a name for the modern age. It should probably not, Hoffer says, be called the age of the masses. A better title would be the age of the intellectual. For the first time in his writings, perhaps because his condemnation of this dangerous person had raised so many eyebrows in academia and elsewhere, Hoffer carefully defines the intellectual. He is "a literate person who feels himself a member of the educated minority" (73). He believes the masses incapable of self-rule, and he believes that he and his elite friends know best what the masses need. He champions the masses but secretly despises them the way a brutal headmaster hates his pupils. He despises the menial task of feeding and clothing people but loves to devise BIG plans for society. In recent years his chances of taking over in this country have greatly improved, and Americans must head him off by raising the educational level of our people so high there will be no elite corps. Where everyone is an intellectual, Hoffer says, there can be no intellectual.

Essay five looks at the recent talk about a return to nature. As a migratory worker, Hoffer had found nature a far cry from hospitable, and he found "nature boy" talk odd. For him the battle between man and nature is the central theme of the great drama of history. According to Hoffer, man became human when he broke with nature, when he became unnatural, and to return him to nature is to dehumanize him. He calls "the city" man's refuge against nature; and he warns against letting cities become uninhabitable. "Both the scientist and the savage postulate the oneness of man and nature," he explains (102). Neither can see the very vital difference between the two. The savage treats nature as man, while the scientist treats man as nature. Man's future hope may lie in his ability to make this distinction.

Essay six tries to define the nature of the modern age. It is foremost a time of impatience, Hoffer says, a time when no one takes the time to grow. Most men would rather die for a cause than work for it. Traditionally American energy has gone to the market place, to business, to industry; but since *Sputnik* the wheeler-dealers have entered academia and have "Europeanized" America. Typically "intellectual," they hate America's earthiness. They think that the mark of a great society is its ability to produce great leaders when in fact the great society is one that can get along quite well without them. But the American masses will resist these new intellectuals, Hoffer optimistically whistles in the dark, and America will remain the best place on earth for the common man.

The Temper of Our Time, though written for others, is vintage Hoffer. It is essential Hoffer. Its message is clear: a free people must reject the overtures of all would-be saviors who tell them their humanness is wrong.

First Things, Last Things (1971)

This book, written in the waning days of the 1960s, is composed of nine essays, several of which were previously published in magazines. They deal mostly with the rise of man's creative urge, with the dangers and potentials of leisure, and with the cities in which both of these fascinating phenomena have always emerged.

In "Man's Most Useful Occupation," which is play, Hoffer says that Paleolithic man's cave drawings, as in the Altamira Caverns, reflect both his admiration for animals superior to himself and the playful spirit that enabled him eventually to surpass them by imitating them. Man survived by his cunning but moved up the evolutionary ladder by his play. The child's pet puppy preceded the hunting dog, the ornament preceded clothing, the musical bow preceded the weapon. Wheels appeared first on toys, then on vehicles to pull loads. Man is still, as he has always been, at his best when he spends his time and energy on the superfluous. Again Hoffer explains that it is man's unfinishedness that makes him perpetually young, always at play, always a creator: "Man first became human in an Eden playground, and how we have a chance to attain our ultimate destiny, our fullest humanness, by returning to the playground" (12).[6]

In "The Birth of Cities," as Hoffer continues to build his myth of man's development, he describes the first walled cities as refuges for the human debris blown away from communal nomadic societies. Life in the earliest cities, as in cities throughout history, reflected the values and personalities of the wandering hunters that composed them: violent, controversial, leisurely, creative. Farming communities, the suburbs of early cities, were from the beginning uncreative bastions of conservatism, manned by people who could not compete in the cities. Significantly, Hoffer points out, the backward countries today are village societies, while the progressive ones are societies of cities.

Responding again to the "back to nature" movement of the late 1960s, Hoffer's third chapter, "Cities and Nature," paints Mother Nature in something less than soft, benign colors. Recalling again his years in the fields, he asserts that man's artificial cities are far superior to life in nature, for cities are refuges from "an inhospitable, nonhuman cosmos" (30). Man became human when he cut himself off and freed himself from nature. This is why in cities, the citadels against nature, man has made all his great achievements. Americans should not fear subduing their continent, he says, but they should fear losing the current battle for their cities. Only in cities can nature's bonds be broken and man be truly free; but only in cities, with their human density, must man do battle with his other enemy, nature within him.

In "The Tilt of the Social Landscape," Hoffer discusses the fact that until recently America's energy and talent flowed to the marketplace. Even potential literary men, men of words, were forced to be businessmen. This was before *Sputnik,* "Khrushchev's Toy," tilted our social landscape and made it possible and profitable for "wheeler-dealers" to climb the academic ladder as scientists. "Men of action cast in the role of men of words," they give off as much energy as men of words cast in the role of men of action once did in American business. In their misplaced search for "relevance" these laboratory supermen have made the American universities un-American, more like French universities, for in France men of words have long been encouraged to be politically active. Hoffer shows that Jews have experienced this phenomenon of misplaced energy since they were driven out of business and into the role of warriors to defend a homeland. America's twentieth century, he says, may well be a "Jewish" century.

In "The Young and the Middle Aged," Hoffer discusses the painful passage modern youth experience trying to become adults. Affluence has robbed them of the need to work which once required them to pursue activity that proved manhood. Hoffer suggests that at puberty every child be put to work cleaning up the nation's cities, proving his manhood. It has only been since the middle-class–inspired industrial revolution, he says, that middle-aged men have controlled society; and only under middle-aged, middle-class leadership have young people been kept sheltered babies. Before the industrial revolution, the world was run by children; and now, in what Hoffer calls the postindustrial age, children are trying once again to take over. The middle class was good at managing things—young people are good, they believe, at managing people. Armed with magical charms, dressed like peacocks, these youthful intellectuals just may turn the United States into a neomedieval society.

In "Whose Country?" Hoffer again explains why intellectuals hate America. They are left alone here, and they hate being left alone. They want to be taken seriously, he says, to make history, and here they are kept from power. Citing as an example Herbert Marcuse, a man who seemed to hate the society of equals that saved him from Nazism, Hoffer says, "Scratch an intellectual and you will find a would-be aristocrat who loathes the sight, the sound and the smell of common folk" (75). America must remain the property of the common people, he roars. They built it. They keep it strong.

But in "The Spirit of an Age," Hoffer mourns the passing of the machine age, when the middle class spent their time managing things and left men alone. The middle class did little to improve man's lot, it is true, but at least its members did not try to control man's mind. Now the middle class, unable to handle contemporary problems, is losing out to younger men who represent preindustrial values, values that encourage them to be saviors of mankind, which means controllers of mankind.

In "Thoughts on the Present," Hoffer mourns the fact that in trying to right wrongs in recent years we have unleashed unbelievable chaos. Young people now want to "teach before they learn, retire before they work, rot before they ripen" (103). They search for good reasons to do bad things. They have begun to "Latin Americanize" the United States because a timid majority is afraid to oppose them. A stable society, Hoffer says, is one that strikes a balance between the demands of a vigorous minority and the rights of a vigorous majority. If American society is to survive, Americans must "be strong and resolute enough to deal swiftly and relentlessly with those who would mistake its good will for weakness" (101). These are strong words from a man thoroughly disgusted with a permissive and therefore chaotic society.

Finally, in "The Madhouse of Change," Hoffer contrasts the European peasant who came to the United States a generation ago with the one who fled to the urban centers of Europe. Here they were reborn, they were made new men, with new names, a new language, a new lease on life. There they could be reborn only by joining a cause and marching in a mass movement. The Negro in Detroit, like the Sicilian in Milan, cannot be reborn. He must absorb all the abuses of change without an escape. Thus the current madhouse in the American cities.

This is a hard-hitting book. It sold well enough, but not as well as Hoffer's earlier books, and found a much less receptive audience because it violated the grazing space of too many contemporary sacred cows.

Reflections on the Human Condition (1973)

Hoffer's seventh book is as exciting and at the same time as difficult to focus as *The Passionate State of Mind.* It is a collection of 183 paragraphs, each one reaching out boldly toward a new idea, loosely organized under five headings. Its overall theme, to be found only by some rather intense reflection on Hoffer's reflections, is the origin and nature of man.

In "Between the Dragon and the Devil," Hoffer expands on his earlier anthropological myth. Man the unfinished animal, nature's mistake, striving always to finish himself, has become nature's adversary. He is dehumanized not by being separated from nature but by being made to act a part of nature, like an animal. To automate man, to make him predictable, is to primitivize him, to make him a part of the very nature he has sought so long to escape.

Hoffer says that while the Eastern world has always honored nature by treating it as a dread enemy, in symbolic art a dragon, the West has broken so free of nature in recent centuries that its enemy is appropriately "nature within," symbolized by the devil. By "playing" with nature, Western man triumphed over it. In our day, however, the fear of a nuclear holocaust has brought the dragon to the West. Hoffer believes that only when we once again become learners, not learned, will we resume our proper relationship with the created order.

In the second section, "Troublemakers," Hoffer paints a gloomy picture of the contemporary scene. A pregnant world writhes in labor while spoiled minorities prepare to rip open its belly. Untalented, alienated groups, led by intellectuals who love madhouses where they can be saviors, look in vain for public cures for private ills. The younger generation, unskilled, caught up in an undefined and seemingly interminable passage to adulthood, fall prey to medicine men loaded with primitive methods of dehumanization. Hoffer is obviously in a state of despair.

In section three, "Creators," he is much more optimistic. Here he speaks of the "learners" he believes are the hope of mankind. Learners, creative people, never stop growing, they are willing to work and be patient until they have reached their goals, and they do not take themselves too seriously. They ask questions and search diligently for answers. They guard the spark of humanness in man. The revolutionary and the creative person are both perpetual juveniles; but the revolutionary remains young because he cannot grow, while the creative person remains young because he cannot stop growing. Creativity, which is not rare the way uncreative intellectuals think, is the music of the stretched soul, the soul in conflict with energies that flow in different directions. Hoffer suggests that we learn to recognize it in the masses, let it come naturally to the surface, and watch it work wonders on all the problems posed by the troublemakers.

Section four, "Prognosticators," is the vaguest and least useful of the sections. The major point is that psychology can tell us more about man than history. History tells us only the various experiments man has tried on man. Psychology tells us of man's future potential.

Section five, "The Individual," is quite pessimistic, and its autobiographical coloring reflects Hoffer's own response to the public disapproval of his statements in the late 1960s. There is malice, he says, in our willingness to overestimate people, for we take great pleasure when they fail to reach our expectations. The person who bites the hand that feeds him, he says, will lick the boot that kicks him. Creeping death, he says, is evident when we cannot praise the living. To grow old, he says, is to grow common. But even amid such thick gloom, Hoffer finds wonder in the autonomous individual. "It is the individual only who is timeless," he says. "The individual's hungers, anxieties, dreams, and preoccupations have remained unchanged through the millennia," and "if in some manner the voice of an individual reaches us from the remotest distance of time, it is a timeless voice speaking about ourselves (97).[7]

Reflections on the Human Condition is not one of Hoffer's best books. Its lasting paragraphs would perhaps occupy the space of a long essay. Yet these paragraphs are among his finest. Hoffer has once again struck sparks to help light up a darkened landscape.

In Our Time (1976)

Hoffer's eighth book, published three years after *Reflections on the Human Condition,* as Hoffer was nearing seventy-five, is far different in tone from its two predecessors. Not only is it a collection of thirty-two very brief essays (which might serve as models for writers entering the Hoffer-Fabilli essay contest he has sponsored at the University of California), but it is almost wholly positive in approach. Hoffer sounds here a bit like a kindly grandfather advising admiring children about the good life: a refreshing change in tone from his recent gloom but perhaps not as philosophically rewarding or even as honest as the old irascible Eric Hoffer.

Here he says America is still the best place on earth for the common man. Here alone he is left alone to realize his potential. America has learned from the terrible decade of the 1960s that affluence is a positive threat to social stability, that adult failure to act in defense of basic rights is more critical than youth's tendency to take them away, that trying to right wrongs is a perilous undertaking, and that a sense of usefulness is more important to people than wealth or even our highly tauted freedom.

Back in the 1960s, Hoffer admits, he often shuddered at the thought of a world run by youth. Now he realizes that most of history has been made by juveniles. He recommends that he start adulthood at thirteen, let people retire at forty, and set "older folks" free to bring about a cultural renaissance. He once again mourns the end of the era of the middle class, when leaders of society loved power and not prestige, and he says that the future will probably be less civil and less humorous than the past, for lovers of money are generally easier taskmasters than haters of money. He fears that the postindustrial age may be as barbarous as the preindustrial one was. But he believes in the future enough to outline plans for new schools in which young people will be taught the skills needed to run the world, in which "dull" work will be seen, as Hoffer always saw it, as an opportunity to think while working. He envisions streets of small shops manned by skilled laborers, after the style of renaissance Florence, where everyone has an opportunity to grow.

There is also here a great deal about the wonders of capitalism, an admission that it cannot help the helpless, a salute to it for the opportunity it gives those who want to help themselves. Hoffer reflects upon communism's ability to help the helpless but not to provide opportunities for the self-sufficient and advises Russia to open up Siberia, as the United States did its middle west, to Russian capitalists. Through all of these essays runs a deep admiration for the trader in history, the man whose heart has always been set on baubles, the man who makes society's least dangerous leader.

Here also Hoffer vents his spleen against his pet peeves: cowardly majorities, "adversary" intellectuals who undermine faith in the very country that protects them, historians who can tell us nothing about the future, social reformers who try to right wrongs without considering the chaos they might bring down on everyone's head, and the myth and prejudice being taught under the name Black Studies. There are some rather intriguing generalizations about China's energy, Russia's stultification, America's inability to experience tragedy, man's capacity for compassion, for shame, and for the rebirth that offers ever-present hope for the future.

All things considered, though, *In Our Time* must be deemed Hoffer's weakest book, weak enough to call into question his continuing worth as a social commentator. Even he admitted, while writing it, that it would be small and tame: "I threw out several strident chapters. I no longer want to bark" (102).[8] And he admitted while he waited for it to be printed that he felt he was scraping the bottom of his barrel. It does contain a few striking ideas and a handful of memorable sentences. It is overall an optimistic book for an old man. It deserves to be part of the Hoffer corpus. But it was soon to be eclipsed by a journal, *Before the Sabbath,* which would prove that Hoffer's decline was temporary.

Before the Sabbath (1979)

This most recent book, the one Hoffer expects to be his final statement before taking his final sabbath of rest, is a journal he kept during the crucial year 1974–75. Feeling that he had scraped bottom, he decided once again, as in 1958–59, to keep a day-by-day record of what he thought as he read and reflected on life. He used the diary as a sluice box, the kind he had used to pan for gold in the California mountains forty years before, to see if he could catch any last drippings from a "shrunken mind" (1–2). The results, severely edited when young Eric protested references to himself and Hoffer granted him permission to escape immortality, surprised everyone, Hoffer included. *Before the Sabbath* proved to be a marvelous book.

It is full of Hoffer's prejudices, blatantly and wonderfully stated. On every page, as one reviewer observes, there is "at least one startling idea."[9] It is a fine book for the reader just discovering the Hoffer feast. There are enough new questions here to keep Hoffer busy thinking and writing for another decade at least, should he decide not to take his sabbatical after all.

There is a Hoffer book yet to be written on the Jews. Here he credits them with creating optimism, fanaticism, and indeed the Western mind (107, 100, 81). His musings about the way the Jews develop differently in different nations ask enough questions to keep a "learning person" busy for a long time (15).

There is a Hoffer book yet to be written about the great cultural ages of the past and the cities that gave them birth. Hoffer is here especially full of speculation about the nature of what he considers the West's golden age, the nineteenth century: its birth in the violence of the Napoleonic era, its domination by middle-class "men of action," its orderliness, its optimism, its naiveté, and its almost total dissimilarity from the twentieth century. Still another book could be dedicated to the nature and destiny of the nineteenth century's economic system, capitalism, its continuing efficiency, its tenacity despite the constant attempts to bring it down.

Hoffer could build from comments in this book another book on old age. Old age is, Hoffer tells us, not a rumor (41). It renders people common (44). It gives one a keener sense of time (130). It can be, if there is no one to care, a time of great sorrow (138); but it also can give one a capacity for enjoying the beautiful things of the world without wanting to possess them (54).

Then there are bits and pieces of ideas so tantalizing that anyone would wish Hoffer another decade to work on them further. Why is it easier to de-Christianize a society than to de-Islamize one? Why does a society grow more repressive with every outside threat to its autonomy? Why is it that the more foreign the influence on a society the more long lasting it proves to be? Hoffer remains, as he nears eighty, a man of untold philosophical challenge.

So the Hoffer library, the wine pressed from a harvest of thought, the nine brief books of distilled essence. Hoffer's work assures us that he will not be forgotten. The man who spent his first fifty years in obscurity will be immortal.

Chapter Five

The Achievement:
The Myth of Man

Casual readers may be tempted to assume that their brief glances through Hoffer's books have acquainted them with the essential Hoffer. The apparently familiar words, the polished, apparently obvious phrases, the direct and apparently simple sentences and paragraphs make Hoffer appear easy. He is not. Appearances, as far as Hoffer is concerned, are highly deceiving. His philosophy can easily be interpreted inadequately and incorrectly; and its deeper implications, without careful reading and reflection, can be missed altogether.

This is true in part because Hoffer uses certain words in his own peculiar way for his own peculiar purposes, in part because his broad comments on a wide range of topics demand more background reading than most readers can claim, in part because his thought is unsystematically scattered over nine books, and few readers have the time or skill to put the pieces together. But it is perhaps true mostly because this skid-row dishwasher, migrant farm laborer, longshoreman, and retired senior citizen draws his conclusions from experiences very few readers can appreciate. Few who share his memories read, and few who read share his memories.

It is, therefore, essential that any book on Hoffer try, as this one will, to present a systematic survey of the central Hoffer themes, which once harmonized form a grand myth of man, the social animal. To do this has meant reading and rereading the Hoffer books, slowly and deliberately organizing the Hoffer themes, eliminating extraneous, peripheral matter, and following the fascinating Hoffer myth from beginning to end. What emerges from such labor is no new gospel to follow or new heresy to be condemned but a feast table crowded with every kind of tempting dish.

Hoffer's great accomplishment, the achievement that makes his name immortal, is his grand myth of man. A myth is of course a story which in concrete terms presents a truth that can be expressed in no other form. Hoffer is a social and political analyst in the tradition of de Tocqueville. He is a gifted essayist in the tradition of Montaigne. But he is first and foremost a mythmaker in the tradition of Thomas Hobbes and John Locke.

He is, unlike any who have come before him, a distinctively American mythmaker. Despite his unusual childhood, in which there was not the usual American public-school experience, despite his preference for French and other European writers, despite a lingering feeling that he is somehow not at home in this country, Hoffer is unashamedly, unequivocally American both in perspective and in attitude. He has been outside the borders of the United States one time and then for about ten minutes; and though he blithely comments on personalities and happenings all over the world, his only real interest is America. "I'm not even very American," he has said. "I don't want the same things they do, I don't worship the same idols, and my experience has been so far removed from theirs. And yet, somehow, there is something deeply American in all my thinking" (*EH,* 5). That something is a fierce pride in the American common man, Hoffer's chief preoccupation, and the nation he has built.

It is perhaps Hoffer's mythmaking, more than anything else, that makes him so easily misunderstood. The mythmaker must feel his way through a maze of puzzles and distractions, through uncharted territory, repeating, reversing, contradicting himself, searching for new ways to express old truths and old ways to express new ones. He must be able to use both tuition and intuition, both his conscious and his unconscious experience, and he must be able to find a universe in every grain of sand. He must work essentially alone, in isolation, free to make the grave errors and grand discoveries that are always made alone, braving all the terrors of solitude that few men have the inner resources to endure. He must be willing to simplify complexities and exaggerate commonplaces, to ride roughshod over consistency's petty fortresses, to categorize and stereotype people and events and break all the nice rules of scholarly tolerance and intolerance.

Hoffer has been willing and able to do these things. He is a brother to Hesiod, the Greek peasant who collected and gave literary shape to the oral myths of Hellas. He is in the fullest sense the American Hesiod, an eternally playful child pointing with undisguised joy at the fascinating myth he has amazed himself by constructing.

With no apology to anthropologists, historians, or theologians, Hoffer has waded off into the primordial swamp to investigate man's origins, the development of his brain and his passions, and the peculiar set of circumstances that made him the only animal capable of individuality. "It is the individual alone who is timeless," Hoffer says. "The individual's hungers, anxieties, dreams, and preoccupations have remained unchanged throughout the millennia."[1] He has examined the effects of change on this individualistic man, how change brings out the creator and the fanatic in him, how he is forced by change to gather with his own kind behind city walls to play with his toys and learn to conquer "nature without" if not always "nature within." He has traced the path of the "man of words" from scribe to writer to rebel, the path of the passionate man through his various stages of true believing, and the path of the man of practical action from his role as early trader to his modern role as capitalist. He has traced the history of the common man through fifty dreary centuries of being used by aristocrats to his one great opportunity to prove himself on a virgin continent in a place called America.

It is wise, when dealing with Hoffer and his myth, to lay aside all assumptions and received wisdom. The response to the man and his myth can be neither "liberal" nor "conservative." It must be creative.

Man

If it is true, as J. P. Mayer has said in his study of Alexis de Tocqueville, that the "riddle of man's nature is the starting point of all political philosophy,"[2] then Hoffer begins at the beginning.

For Hoffer, man's uniqueness, all that is both frightening and marvelous about him, lies in his unfinishedness. God (or Nature, depending on which Hoffer essay one reads) first made a fully automated world, both animate and inanimate, one that worked perfectly with or without him; but after a time he grew weary of his world's monotony and began to play, to tinker with his creation. From his tinkering came man, a "runaway experiment," an animal without instinct but with a wonderful mind and a free will.[3] The God who created the world was a great technician, Hoffer says, but the God who created man was an artist, and he created man in his own image. "All other animals are perfect technicians, each with its built-in tool kit, each an accomplished specialist," Hoffer explains. "Man is a technically misbegotten creature, half finished and ill-equipped, but in his mind and soul are all the ingredients of a creator, of an artist." For Hoffer, it is "God's mark as a supreme artist that he refused to automate man," (*EH,* 19). From the beginning, then, man was the creature to watch.

Since man had no specialized organs, no built-in tool kit, to protect him from his enemies and assure his survival, he was forced to depend on his wits. He greatly admired and envied the other animals, his superiors in the natural world. "There is a perfect ant, a perfect bee, but man is perpetually unfinished," Hoffer says. "There is something unhuman about perfection. They who would make man perfect end up dehumanizing him."[4] "It is this incurable unfinishedness which sets man apart from other living things."[5] So man watched with envious admiration the more serious, better equipped animals around him; and all of his inventions—his dances, his painting, even his clothing—were byproducts of his attempts to imitate and thereby raise himself to equality with them:

He became Homo Faber—a maker of weapons and tools—to compensate for his lack of specialized organs. He became Homo Ludens—a player, tinkerer, and artist—to compensate for his lack of inborn skills. He became a speaking animal to compensate for his lack of the telepathic faculty by which animals communicate with each other. He became a thinker to compensate for the ineffectualness of his instincts.[6]

The weak, unfinished animal called man did, Hoffer says, have a special gift, perhaps an accident of God's tinkering, a "seminal pause of hesitation,"[7] a capacity for reflective reasoning when a danger or problem presented itself and no instinctual response appeared to give direction. "This pause," Hoffer says, "is a seedbed of the apprehensions, the insights, the images, and the concepts which are the warp and woof of the creative process."[8] Only man among the animals had the capacity for creative reflection, and only the particular individual men and women who had it in sufficient supply survived to become the fathers and mothers of the human species.

Man's reflective reason, Hoffer believes, helped him eventually subdue and triumph over the other animals and even nature itself. It enabled him to build artificial organs to compensate for his natural deficiencies, and it gave him the technology necessary to break nature's iron laws and remake the world to suit himself. Man, Hoffer says with a flourish, was nature's (God's) greatest mistake. For not perfecting him, for not making him dull and humorless and efficient, nature has been paying ever since: "For in the process of finishing himself man got out from underneath nature's inexorable laws, and became her most formidable adversary."[9]

Because man is unfinished, Hoffer explains, he always keeps growing. He cannot grow up. He is a perpetual juvenile, "the only young thing in the world. . . . A deadly seriousness emanates from all other forms of life. The cry of pain and of fear man has in common with other living things, but he alone can smile and laugh" (*EH*, 2). Despite his weakness and insecurity, his lingering feeling of inferiority, his suspicion that he is not native to this world, he remains lighthearted, playful, childlike, always tinkering with his toys. Speaking of earliest man, Hoffer says:

All around him were living creatures superbly equipped, and driven by grim purposefulness. He alone, with childlike carelessness, tinkered and played, and exerted himself more in the pursuit of superfluities than of necessities.[10]

From his tinkering came the inventions that would make him supreme in the world. Play was and still is his most useful occupation.

The wheel, the bow, and most other practical devices were first toys. "Man was shaped less by what he had to do than by what he did in playful moments" (*EH,* 13). His tinkering and playing, his imitation of his creator, "were a chief source of the inventiveness which enabled man to prevail over better-equipped and more purposeful animals."[11] His childlikeness survives today in two of the most interesting of human types: "Both the revolutionary and the creative individual are perpetual juveniles. The revolutionary does not grow up because he cannot grow, while the creative individual cannot grow up because he keeps growing" (*EH,* 12).

Insecure, playful man, Hoffer says, was able to cut himself off from a hostile nature and become human. History is then for Hoffer the story of humanization, "of man's torturous ascent through the millennia, of his ceaseless effort to break away from the rest of the creation and become an order apart" (*EH,* 7). This is why "man is an eternal stranger in this world. He became a stranger when he cut himself off from the rest of creation and became human."[12] Humanization for Hoffer is the process of gaining freedom from nature. Dehumanization is the reclamation of man by nature: "Man became what he is not with the aid, but in spite, of nature."[13] To control man, the forces of tyranny must fit him into the predictable mold of the natural world, and man always resists, knowing without knowing how he knows that his humanity is being taken from him.

Hoffer credits the biblical Hebrews with having first "enunciated a clear-cut separation between man and nature." They were the first to see that man is truly unique, that his uniqueness puts him into direct conflict with the natural world, that Adam must subdue Adama or be subdued, that in the human order it is Jacob (not the "natural" man Esau) who must be patriarch of the new race. Hoffer sees the myth of the expulsion from paradise as a narrative of man's break with nature. By imitating and thus threatening his creator (God/Nature), man got himself "bounced" from the "garden" but freed himself from the iron law of necessity, took God/Nature on as an adversary, and vowed one day to return to storm the place.[14]

From the strange dilemma of being in a world but not part of it, Hoffer says, "stem our incurable insecurity, our unfulfillable craving for roots, our passion to cover the world with man-made compounds, our need for a God who appoints us His viceroy on earth" (*EH,* 10). Man prays to and abases himself before the very God he considers an adversary, and his contradictory behavior generates tremendous energy. Hoffer believes that "anytime we try the untried, turn a dream into reality, overcome insurmountable obstacles, we are in some measure sharing God's style."[15] A bit more cynically he says, "God is man's greatest invention. Man shapes Him in the image of what he wants to be, and then defeats him."[16]

Slowly, imitating and competing with his God, man began learning universal laws. Slowly, then more rapidly, he moved toward the first machine age, the late Neolithic period, the time of the first cities, the time the Hebrew Bible symbolized with the tower of Babel. The first machine age was a failure, a "confusion of tongues," because man was still unable to cooperate through communication.[17]

After the first failure, Hoffer says, there followed nearly six thousand years of tedious struggle upward to a second machine age. Always going before man, leading him onward, was the Hebrew-Christian God, the Creator of Nature, its Lawgiver, the Machine Maker Supreme—a figure to be admired, feared, imitated, surpassed, conquered. Just two centuries ago the second machine age began. Its machines were at first only half effective. They would go only if men were strapped to them. They were like the Bull of Pharsalis which could make its screaming growls only when men were thrust inside its flaming belly. Then, only yesterday, from sparkling laboratories, came the automation that would free man from labor and enable him finally to conquer his old enemy nature. Now man stands once again at the gates of Eden, grimy, caked with sweat, still unsure of himself, but now capable of storming the old citadel and taking his rightful place in the ultimate sabbath of rest.

But this is getting ahead of the story—and passing over some very important parts. The climb toward the first machine age was as slow and torturous as the second one. Earliest man's insecurity led him first to form corporate societies, nomadic but secure, which filled both his psychological and his physical needs. Man was not, in fact, an autonomous individual then. He had a place, a function, a purpose. He knew shame if and when he violated the corporate code, but he never knew the guilt of an autonomous individual.[18]

Man's City

It was only as the last ice age ended, Hoffer says, that the corporate, nomadic societies began to crack. Changes in the northern hemisphere's climate ended the easy hunting and grain gathering of earlier days, and the corporate communities were no longer as secure or as able to shelter all their members. Change drove certain individuals out into a hostile world and made them wandering misfits. The winds of change blew them like so much human debris over the landscape until at last, in various parts of the near east, they began to gather behind stockade walls to form man's first cities.[19]

The first city dwellers, according to Hoffer, were the desperately insecure and passionate victims of change. They were (and are in every age's cities) potentially both highly creative and highly destructive. They were and are the volatile products of broken habits that can be "more painful and crippling than broken bones" and of disintegrating values that "may have as deadly a fallout as disintegrating atoms."[20] Change cracked the communal framework of primitive society, and passionate city life was born, as is always the case when change works its will.[21]

Hoffer explains that what the early misfits needed most of all, and what misfits of every age need most, was an opportunity to prove their personal worth, to prove that even without the designated role of corporate society they had value. Hoffer compares sixteenth-century Europe and twentieth-century Asia, two societies similar in their frantic efforts to survive change, communal societies broken open and spilling out misfits. Sixteenth-century Europe had a newly discovered America to conquer, a perfect battleground for the passionate individuals to prove their worth; twentieth-century Asia has no place for this individual to go and nothing for him to do. Sixteenth-century Europe avoided self-destructive social revolution; twentieth-century Asia has and will not. The passion to excel, says Hoffer, a passion found in cities among misfits, is always born of the insecurity that comes from a crisis of self-esteem. The person forced to be an autonomous individual tries with all his might to persuade others of his personal value because he must persuade himself.[22]

What he needs most, what satisfies his inner longings most completely, is a new birth to a new personal identity.[23] If he finds some way to become a new person, if he is given an opportunity to excel under a new identity, this passionate individual can become extremely creative. If a new birth to a new identity in a new country is not possible, the passionate individual is ripe for conversion to a cause of one kind or another. Hoffer here compares the Europeans who came to America and with new names, a new language, sometimes even a new religion, were given a chance to conquer a new land to the Europeans who remained in the old country and joined the Nazis and Fascists. This is why modern Asia is so ready to go Marxist. There is a juvenile quality, a bitter in-betweenness, about the man rendered autonomous by change. Caught in the ordeal of change, he entertains wild dreams, tells extravagant fairy tales, participates in gigantic masquerades and preposterous pretensions, and readily falls into step behind passionate messiahs leading mass migrations to promised lands. Marxism, as did other mass movements before it, offers such dreams, masquerades, and migrations.[24]

The explosive debris stirred up by change, Hoffer explains, gathered and still gathers in stockades. The first time this happened, four thousand years ago, the first cities were born. The misfits fought, but they also learned from each other, and together they built up grand myths and built toys to amuse themselves. The life of cities, Hoffer says, has always had about it a "hunter" quality—full of violence and creative tinkering, debate and sharing. Behind their walls, during lulls in raids on other cities or hunting seasons, the first city dwellers, like their modern counterparts, invented the machines that eventually enabled them to conquer the world that had frightened them into their walls. Man's greatest achievements came not in deserts or mountaintops but in crowded, noisy, smelly cities. Says Hoffer:

The birth of the city was a crucial step in man's separation from nature. The city cut man off not only from the non-human cosmos but also from clans, tribes, and other primitive modes of organization. A self-governing city populated by more or less autonomous individuals has been the cradle of freedom, art, literature, science, and technology.[25]

As in all of the ages since, Hoffer says, much of the actual inventing was done by men the natural world outside the walls would have called weak and undesirable. "Indeed, the formidableness of the human species stems from the survival of its weak. Were it not for the compassion that moves in to care for the sick, the crippled, and the old there probably would have been neither culture nor civilization."[26] The crippled warrior, no longer able to fight, became and becomes the storyteller, the teacher, the artisan. The aged and the dyspeptic became and becomes the healer and the cook. Music and philosophy were and are composed and written by unhappy men whose taut heart strings are pulled between passionate minds and unresponsive bodies, or vice versa. The weak, the undesirables, full of the self-hate that begets passion, little tied to the recurrent rhythms of nature, blaze the paths on which subsequent generations walk into the future. "One thinks of the venerable sage, the unhinged medicine man, the epileptic prophet, the blind bard, and the witty hunchback and dwarf."[27] Indeed, "one is justified in fearing that the elimination of the weak as shaping factors" in our own age "may mean the end of history—the reversion of history to zoology."[28]

The weak, Hoffer believes, are man's creative pioneers because "when a situation is so unprecedented that no amount of knowledge or experience is adequate to master it," those limited by experience are more fit to deal with it than those who consider themselves learned. "The unknown and untried give as it were a special fitness to the unfit." Thus "the difficult and risky task of meeting and mastering the new" is always undertaken by a society's misfits, failures, fugitives, outcasts and their like."[29] Only in the city could the weak survive and find fertile soil for their ideas.

The city, however, was and is not a utopia. While it insulates man from nature without, thus giving him a chance to become more human, it concentrates in a very limited space man's own nature, "nature within" as Hoffer calls it, which can be even worse than nature without. Man's fatal tendency to passionate fanaticism is encouraged in the city. The uprooted city dweller of every age is prey to "medicine men" who would turn him into a true believer in a holy cause. "We have mastered nature outside the city," Hoffer says, "only to find that it has invaded the city and turned it into a jungle."[30] In the city "man's lusts and fears have free play, and dehumanization spreads like the plague." In the city "this lust finds the human material to work on."[31] Yet Hoffer himself would live no other place; for the city, despite its dangers, is man's optimal creative milieu. "Man's greatest achievements," he says, "were conceived and realized not in the bracing atmosphere of plains, deserts, forests and mountaintops but in the crowded, noisy and smelly cities."[32]

Hoffer believes, in light of the tragic events of the 1960s, that nature within caused man's earliest cities, where he had reached his highest technological advancement, to decline and fall. Only the suburban villages that surrounded the dying cities, inhabitated by dull and uncreative men who could not compete in the cities, survived to keep the cities' inventions alive until the next cities could rise and take them all a step further. While the villages that fill the spaces between the rise of cities are transmitters of technological culture, only in the cities, beginning with those of the Sumerian hunters, does man take giant strides forward.[33]

Hoffer's attitude toward nature (and the "nature boys" who want to return modern man to it) grew out of his years in the fields when he had to fight nature every step of his way. He says he always felt more human walking down a blacktop road toward a town than walking in a field where brambles cut his hands and tripped his feet. America's Romantic view of nature he finds amusing because it is rooted not in the obviously hostile milieu of North America but is borrowed from the literature of a mild continent called Europe. He laughs about Berkeley students who read Wordsworth, go up into the California hills to make love, and come home with poison oak. Once when he found a milkweed plant growing from a crack in front of an abandoned storefront in San Francisco, he wrote that he had uncovered a vanguard spy of aggressive nature, casing the joint for a coming reinvasion. One of his favorite places on earth is Golden Gate Park, where man has used nature to make a very human place. Every tree and plant is told where and how to grow, subject to the will of man, completely artificial, thoroughly beautiful, and this is how things should be.

Nature, both without and within, is always threatening to return man to his primeval past. His future, his hope, lies in cities. Despite their shortcomings, they are the places where men learn from each other how to live in the future. If cities are lost, all is lost.[34] Of America specifically, Hoffer says: "If this country declines and decays it will be not because we have raped and ravaged a continent, but because we do not know how to build and maintain viable cities."[35]

Scribe, Writer, Rebel

To be found within man's cities, from the very beginning, were the same "types" of man Hoffer sees making history in every age. The first "type" was the "man of practical action" who quite early learned to use the toys playful men made to organize and run society. The man of practical action is somewhat dull. He is more a "natural" man than the creative, passionate misfits who perform the function of pioneers; but he runs society in an efficient way. It is this man of practical action who created that eternal "man of words," Hoffer's "intellectual," the scribe.

The man of words, the early scribe, Hoffer says, was first a keeper of books. He kept records, took dictation, and copied documents. His precious skill was much in demand in the early kingdoms and empires (as also later in the Middle Ages), and he was rewarded with food, housing, and a place of importance in the halls of state. His advice was solicited and heeded. The man of the pen rode proudly beside the man of the whip. He never questioned the status quo or doubted the legitimacy of established regimes. His style of life and therefore his attitudes toward life changed only when the societies where he was so highly honored changed. At times the collapse of a kingdom—Sumer, Egypt's Old Kingdom, the Jewish state of Solomon, Agamemnon's Mycenae—brought him down. At times the spread of literacy rendered him common and useless.[36]

Either way, Hoffer says, the out-of-work scribe, unneeded and unwanted, became a writer. He used his scribe's skills to capture the oral ballads of illiterate bards and make them his own expressions of grief and outrage at his new condition. He became an entertainer, a teacher, a sage. If he found success, an audience, loyal disciples, he felt fulfilled and continued to write on and on through his life, creating a literary tradition for his race. Always a lover of words, the scribe turned writer has always preferred the appearance of power to power itself.

Only if he found himself without true creative skills, only if his lamentations of woe and songs of hope brought him no honor and no fame, did he develop the frustrated, passionate nature (a desire to prove his worth) and use his pedestrian skills to the spread of chaos. The scribe turned writer then turned rebel. He used his words to provoke action. He longed to see change that would restore him to his old place of honor. "The scribe ancestry of the revolutionary manifests itself," Hoffer says, "in the fact that when he comes into power he creates a social pattern ideally suited to the aspirations and talents of the scribe—a regimented social order planned, managed, and supervised by a horde of clerks."[37] Those who know they are growing have patience, while those who know they are not growing turn to frenzied effort. Untalented men of words, Hoffer believes, have always longed to make history, to bring word and deed together, to convert complicated, abstract ideas into simple, evocative phrases. (Editor's note: A practice especially noticeable in Soviet Russian agit-prop films.) They have used words to justify all manner of evil. Society's most critical problem has for centuries been how to handle its untalented elitists, its frustrated intellectuals, how to use their considerable energies while keeping them powerless, how to make and keep them paper tigers.(*EH,* 21).

Hoffer is himself a lover of words, and he understands men of words, but he would deny vigorously that he is an intellectual. He would say that he has never been a scribe, never anyone's well-fed and well-scrubbed honored servant, never even financially dependent on his pen. He would say he has never had a grievance against society, never blamed anyone or any thing for his circumstances, never sought literary honors. He would say he has never wanted to direct the affairs of other men, never lusted after the power to control men's destinities. Yet Hoffer is enough a man of words to understand and see the potential dangers in the wordmanship of the intellectual. It is, as he says, only when we see through ourselves that we can see through others.

Mass Movements

Hoffer's unique perspective, as an intelligent nonintellectual and perhaps even antiintellectual, has helped him understand as perhaps no previous writer ever has the dynamics of the varied and sundry mass movements which have captured the attention and claimed the hearts of so many men and changed the course of history so many times through the centuries. As Hoffer puts it in *The True Believer,* mass movements are pioneered by men of words, materialized by fanatics (or true believers), and institutionalized, sanitized, sterilized by men of practical affairs. Since this is probably Hoffer's most significant contribution to the history of thought, we would do well to examine his analysis of mass movements in some detail.

Hoffer says that the uncreative man of words, frustrated by lack of recognition, quite often uses his words to undermine existing institutions by familiarizing the heretofore lethargic masses the ruler hopes to keep cowed with the need for and possibility of change. He creates dissatisfaction by transferring his own inner dissatisfaction to the general public, or to at least enough of it that a movement against the establishment can begin. He prepares the masses for the advent of a new faith. But the man of words, Hoffer says, has always had more vanity than ambition. He creates chaos but shies away from leading a movement that thrives on chaos. He lacks the courage and will to dirty his hands in the very movement his writings have created.

When the egg he has laid is ripe for hatching (Erasmus and Luther of sixteenth-century Europe come to mind) the movement which the man of words has started is taken over by a new type of man, one better equipped to lead it through its active phase, the fanatic. The fanatic loves chaos as much as the intellectual disdains it. It is his true element. He is an even more uncreative man of words than the intellectual. He cannot even create the conditions necessary for the rise of his own movement. But once it has begun, he is indispensable to its continuing development. He is a misfit, a product of change. He feels worthless, and in his lust for pride he is passionate, reckless, ready and willing to sacrifice his hated self to a great cause. "Every extreme attitude," Hoffer explains, "is a flight from self."[38] The fanatic's craving to change the world is in reality a craving to change himself. He wants to see himself as an instrument in the hands of some one or some thing higher than himself. As Hoffer explains it:

Both the strong and the weak grasp at this alibi. The latter hide their malevolence under the virtue of obedience: they acted dishonorably because they had to obey orders. The strong, too, claim absolution by proclaiming themselves the chosen instrument of a higher power—God, history, fate, nation or humanity.[39]

The fanatic, weak or strong, joins a cause in order to lose himself. He is reborn to a new identity, and he convinces himself that he is what he is not. The louder he proclaims his new faith the more one may be sure he needs to convince himself of it. Since he is sick himself, he wants the world to be sick as well, and he wants to be its physician. He claims to be his brother's keeper, but he ends up being his jailer. Proclaiming the brotherhood of man, he fights every battle as if it were a civil war.

Most of the fanatics who join mass movements end up as true-believing foot soldiers, but the particularly gifted may become a general. His is the duty and privilege of molding into a passionate army the host of other misfits who are willing to trade individuality for group pride. He directs and justifies their actions. The more he personally despises them, the more he wants to turn them into efficient machines, the better suited he is to be their leader. "Drastic change," Hoffer says, "creates a proclivity for fanatical attitudes, united actions, and spectacular manifestations of flouting and defiance . . . it creates an atmosphere of revolution."[40] It is within this atmosphere that the fanatic can recruit and lead his army of true believers.

If he is to be successful, if he is to bring the revolution to fruition, the fanatic must do at least eight things for his troops of restless, ruthless, credulous, self-righteous children: (1) He must provide a bold image for them to imitate. (2) He must coerce the fainthearted. (3) He must provide and create a group identity in which the individual without self-esteem can find group pride. (4) He must create a doctrine, a body of beliefs, that insulate the true believers from themselves and from the realities of the present day. (5) He must create a grand drama, a pageant really, of make-believe in which his children have a chance to act out their fantasies. (6) He must also create a spirit of suspicion, a unity of hatred, hatred of enemies outside and traitors within. (7) He must communicate his dreams of a future far different from the present. And with all these things, (8) he must provide his army with constant opportunities to act, to avoid at all costs the boredom that leads to dissatisfaction or the leisure that leads to reflection.[41] The one thing he cannot, and dares not, provide is compassion. Mass movements, Hoffer explains, run on passion, which is a kind of poison, and compassion is an antitoxin. It is the only human quality that cannot be made a fuel for mass action, the only one capable of breaking up a mass movement.[42]

Hoffer points out that the active period of a mass movement, the period when the fanatic is in charge, is invariably a culturally sterile time, certainly not a time of great creativity. Only the most simplistic ideas may be expressed. The man of words who gave birth to the movement seldom survives this period. Through exile or execution he becomes a victim of his own discontent (e.g., Marx). But the active phase is usually relatively brief. Such passion and pageantry as it demands cannot long be sustained. Either the leader is eliminated by the growing cadres of bureaucrats desiring a more tranquil atmosphere in which to pursue their careers or the movement commits suicide in the excesses of its own passions.

Either way the movement is sooner or later captured by the man (sometimes men) of practical affairs, the very kind that ran the society before the man of words precipitated cataclysm. The task of the man of practical affairs and action is to consolidate the fanatic's victories and save the movement from self-destruction. In saving it he usually also takes away its soul. His philosophy is eclectic, his programs pragmatic. He attracts and directs not fanatics but dull career men who make society dull and efficient. It is easy to see why this man always emerges to halt the active phase of a revolution, why he rules so well for so long, and why eventually a new generation of unappreciated men of words come to hate him as the symbol of an unappreciative society and turn the masses against him, thus giving birth to still another mass movement and its revolution.[43]

It is not at all difficult, after Hoffer has shown it to us, to see this very scheme of personalities and events at work in the French and Russian, and to a lesser extent in the Chinese and American, revolutions. Voltaire, Robespierre, Napoleon. Marx, Lenin, Stalin. Sun, Mao, Teng. Sam Adams, Jefferson, John Adams. While in no case, not even the Nazi or Fascist movements, do Hoffer's stereotypes fit neatly the historical patterns, they do help explain causes, dynamics, and consequences. His schema seems to fit the mass movements of modern industrial nations better than those of the emerging third world; but even in modern Africa and Asia, amid all the local peculiarities, the Hofferian models are at work.

The Intellectual

Hoffer's detailed study of the period 1930–1970 led him to go back in time to search for the origins of the scribe-writer-rebel, the man of words, the intellectual, who has played such a significant part in the mass movements of history. The intellectual has in fact been Hoffer's pet peeve for thirty or more years, throughout his writing career. In the preface to *Working and Thinking on the Waterfront,* perhaps because he had been questioned so often about his antipathy to "the very type of person" who presumably bought his books, he attempted to define the intellectual. An intellectual, he said, is one who feels himself a member of an educated minority with the God-given authority to direct and shape events. "An intellectual need not be well educated or particularly intelligent. What counts is the feeling of being a member of an educated elite," he wrote in *Working and Thinking on the Waterfront* (x). He admitted later in the book (64) that he has often been careless about distinguishing the various types of intellectuals; but he still felt that they all share certain common characteristics.

The intellectual, he says in a number of places, prefers a society run by aristocrats, even when the aristocracy persecutes him, to a democratic society like America, where he is unneeded and therefore ignored. America is too "common" for the intellectual, and this is why he feels so uncomfortable here and spends all his time complaining. "Scratch an intellectual and you will find a would-be aristocrat who loathes the sight, the sound and the smell of common folk," Hoffer laughs.[44] The intellectual "has managed to thrive in social orders dominated by kings, nobles, priests, and merchants, but not in societies suffused with the tastes and values of the masses."[45]

The intellectual, Hoffer says, loved the Middle Ages, that golden time when his skills were rare and he held a superior status in a society of well-established and clearly defined classes. This is why the intellectual is constantly trying to restore a medieval society in the modern age, a society in which a secular church and a clerical hierarchy are "served by a population of serfs cowed by doctrinaire double talk."[46] The intellectual, says Hoffer, will "feel at home where an exclusive elite is in charge of affairs, and it matters not whether it be an elite of aristocrats, soldiers, merchants, or intellectuals." He would probably prefer that the elite be literate, but he can put up with one that is not. The only society he cannot abide is one dominated by common people. "There is nothing he loathes more than government of and by the people (*EH*,3). Thus his attitude toward America, where there is too great a dissemination of education and power, where he is unneeded, where he is left alone to stew in his own juices.[47]

The modern intellectual, according to Hoffer, emerged at the end of the renaissance, when literacy spread and put him out of business and has caused every upheaval in the world for the past four hundred years.[48] He does not really love the masses he pretends to champion. He simply needs their worship and the power they can give him. He uses them to give flesh to his grand schemes for the perfection of human society, but once in power his persuasive words turn to orders. He insists mankind is sick, and once he gets man strapped down he operates "with an axe."[49]

The intellectual in every age, Hoffer says, wants above all other things to be heard, to be taken seriously, to be influential. He prefers importance to freedom, persecution even to being left alone. Again this is why the American intellectual (until quite recently a contradiction in terms) is so critical of this country where he is free and envies his brothers living and suffering gloriously under Marxism.[50]

The intellectual, Hoffer says, is at heart a schoolmaster. He does not need to learn any more because he considers himself "learned," and since he is "learned" he longs to teach, to indoctrinate, to arrange the way men think. He turns his society into one huge classroom and gives four-hour lectures. He wonders why his pupils do not work as hard as men work under capitalism, where rewards are so vulgar. Because his own talent is so meager, he fails to see that the masses of common men are lumpy with it.[51]

Instead, he goes forth with his blighted dream of perfecting men and society, dehumanizing, making men into predictable machines that he can control. "To an intellectual," Hoffer says, "power means power over men. He cannot conceive of power moving mountains and telling rivers where to flow. He is in his element commanding, brain washing, and in general making people love what they hate."[52] So, Hoffer concludes, "the savior who wants to turn men into angels is as much a hater of human nature as the totalitarian despot who wants to turn them into puppets."[53] Even "the noble carpenter of Galilee" was a victim of the "solemn scholars, hair-splitting lawyers, and arrogant pedants" of his day.[54] The masses are right to distrust the intellectual, to be antiintellectual. Only the intellectual would define antiintellectualism as a refusal to think.

Hoffer believes that America's relatively stable political history is due to the fact that common men, not intellectuals, have made most of it. 'The masses," he says, if left alone, "are the protagonists of stability, continuity, and law and order."[55] But he says that with the launching of *Sputnik* in 1957, with the subsequent massive federal grants to education aimed at restoring the United States to scientific supremacy, a tilt in the social landscape for the first time brought intellectuals to power in this country. Traditionally young Americans, even those who by natural inclination have become poets and scholars, were drawn to the marketplace, making American business and industry jump with creative electricity. Now, instead of men of words being pressed into action, men of action were being pressed into the academic world; and this led to a new kind of explosion. Laboratory supermen dictating opinion to juveniles, men of action frustrated by the necessarily leisurely pace of university life, longing to move mountains, these displaced persons have precipitated a massive social upheaval.[56] The education explosion of the 1960s has swamped the United States with "hoards of educated nobodies who want to be somebodies and end up being mischief-making busybodies."[57]

The key to the intellectual's mind and his actions, Hoffer believes, is his elitism. "Maybe I should admire them since they have done so much good," Hoffer once said of his colleagues at Berkeley, "but anyone who wants to be a member of an elite goes against my grain."[58] He does not propose that America wipe out its intellectual elite. He would simply like to see America's educational level raised so high that everyone and, therefore, no one would be an intellectual. Society should become a school, he explains, divided into small districts, with everyone continually learning from everyone else. The man who insists he is a member of the educated elite, the intellectual, should be used, his energies should be tapped, but he should never be given power. As Hoffer says, he must be kept a paper tiger.

America

Although Hoffer has spent a great amount of his time and energy on European affairs and so many of his models are foreign, America is at the heart of his work. It is America's uniqueness, the fact that few of his prototypical patterns do not work here, that fascinates him. Hoffer, the son of recently arrived German immigrants, the blind boy who never attended public school, the migrant who still speaks with a thick accent, has always felt both a stranger and perfectly at home here. He can say of the United States what de Tocqueville said of the French aristocracy that he was about to analyze: "I was near enough to know it thoroughly, and far enough to judge it dispassionately."[59]

Hoffer admits that America began not as a haven for the common man but as a series of plantations for aristocrats. The founding fathers were in fact such gentlemen that they did not even kill each other off the way revolutionaries generally do after victory is assured. For the first half century or more after independence most of America's energies still flowed to gentlemanly professions like education, the ministry, and farming. What Hoffer calls the real American revolution, the one that formed his America, arrived in the mid-nineteenth century, when the modern machine age began drawing energy into the marketplace and the new wave of immigrants began arriving from Europe to supply muscle for the industrial age.

This "energizing displacement" of talent from the professions and farms to business and factories, similar to contemporary displacements in Japan (warriors to merchants) and in Israel (merchants to warriors), precipitated the economic and social explosion mentioned earlier. The whole affair was generally opposed by the higher aristocracy because it was such an obvious threat to the old patterns of life, and so it was captured and dominated by "middlebrows," by men with moderate education and social position, men with more freedom to take advantage of change than their "superior" cousins. The nineteenth century, Hoffer explains, became the age of men of practical affairs.

The tug-of-war that continued for another century between "scribe" and "trader" was good for the nation. Warriors and traders can and do reverse roles fairly easily, Hoffer says, and when they do the result is usually an abundance of innovative energy; but scribes (men of words) and traders (men of action) are irreconcilably irreversible and locked in eternal conflict. The scribe passionately seeks to separate the trader from his money, while the trader spreads the scribe's learning to the wider populace. This tug of war between the older aristocracy (men of words) and the new bourgeosie (men of action) created the America of prosperity and democracy.[60]

By 1850, Hoffer says, middlebrow traders ran American society. They were middle-aged men, not boys as the rulers of society had been earlier, and they were hungry not for control of men but for control of industry.[61] Hoffer paraphrases Saint Simon to the effect that the industrial age saw the management of men become the management of things. The new commercial class, with few ideals and almost no ideology, preferred accumulating toys to directing the souls of men. According to Hoffer, it is much "better to be bossed by men of little faith, who have set their hearts on toys, than by men animated by lofty ideals who are ready to sacrifice themselves and others for a cause."[62] He believes America is in some danger now that such men have lost control.

The one great gift (perhaps passion) of the middlebrow American capitalists who built factories and created Hoffer's America was maintenance. These men, unsophisticated and dull as they were, knew how to keep the machines running and saw to it that everything was in its proper place. Hoffer has said that he knew which European nations would recover first from the devastation of World War II: the ones that loved order and respected the virtues of maintenance. He advises anyone who wants to know whether a certain warehouse is efficiently managed to look and see if there is a special nail for the broom. That nail, he says, is "the nail of immortality."[63]

Into the new age dominated by men with hearts set on toys, Hoffer goes on, came millions of European immigrants, outcasts, misfits. Here they were used and often abused by careless bosses and their mindless machines, but here too they were given their first taste of personal freedom in a society run by men who had no interest in managing their souls. Tramps were shown a great continent and told to prove themselves. For the first time in the fifty centuries of human history, Hoffer says, the masses were given an opportunity to demonstrate their worth. They became the pioneers, the path finders, of the American society that would be the envy of the world.[64]

America then is the only country to be shaped by the will and desire of common men. "How can America be so great?" Hoffer teases. "It was created by the scum of the earth."[65] His answer is that the masses, far from being ungifted, are lumpy with talent. All they have always needed was a chance to prove themselves, and that chance came in America. "America was not America until the masses took over," Hoffer says. "Before that, you had a bunch of snobs running it." He gives the aristocratic founding fathers little credit for America's greatness. America is for him the product of common men making their own way. "We came in with Lincoln," Hoffer says.[66] And for the common man, America is the last chance.

Hoffer fairly glories in America's commonness; and he takes shameless pride in the capitalism that gave the American masses their chance to succeed. His greatest fear is that in the post-*Sputnik* age the intellectuals, the old aristocrats, are regaining control. He is afraid that the glorious nineteenth century was a historical deviation and that we may be curving back to earlier days, days of human management. He warns that "the end of the trivial, mean-souled middle class that would sell its soul for cash will probably mean the end of civility, of tolerance, and perhaps of laughter."[67] The twentieth century could well see a return to earlier ages, to primitiveness, to the rule of medicine men and the control of the masses by magic. But Hoffer's pessimism, most evident in the late 1960s and early 1970s, has in more recent years begun to give way to cautious optimism. He has begun to say that the 1980s may see still another tilt in the social landscape. Men of words may again be drawn back to the marketplace as they were in the 1840s. This would mean not only a new economic explosion but also a marked decline in attempts to control the hearts and minds of common men.[68] Once again, as in the past, America would become a land where one could learn, find freedom, and make money, but not gain power over other men.

In his later books, after he has traced the roots of America's greatness, after he has agonized over America's present dilemmas, Hoffer tries to describe the kind of country he would like America to be in the future. It must, if it is to remain great, continue to be the fatherland of common people; and it must become a school in which every man is permitted and encouraged to reach his highest potential. He even suggests creating an experimental pilot State of the Unemployed in which every resident would be both pupil and teacher.[69] "America can be changed into an intellectual, creative, leisure-oriented society," he says, only "when the man who writes books need not feel infinitely superior to the man who . . . binds the books."[70] Hoffer's goal, as he puts it, is to create "a mass elite."[71]

To Hoffer a good society "is a society in which most people have elbow room and the desire to learn and grow," a society where schools produce not learned but learning people, a society in which "the people have neither the time nor the inclination to exploit and oppress, and cannot be tempted to pursue substitutes for growth such as wealth and power."[72] Such a society, he believes, must be rooted in compassion. Almost all noble human qualities, courage, honor, love, hope, faith, duty, and loyalty, "can be transmuted into ruthlessness. Compassion alone stands apart from the continuous

traffic between good and evil proceeding within us. Compassion is
the antitoxin of the soul."[73] Compassion, Hoffer believes, was born
in the family, and he suggests that as the family unit weakens in
modern society compassion could just leak out into the general
society. "I've never been a teacher or a parent," he says, "and my
heart is savage by nature and therefore unfit to tell people how to
implant compassion"; but he believes it might help if every American remembers that we are all together on a tiny speck of earth,
taking a common ride to death.[74] Then perhaps we can stop running
after things we no longer really want.

Music of the Myth

As we noted at the beginning of this chapter, Hoffer's grand
myth of man was constructed block by block over a very long period
of time. He has always permitted himself to chase his dancing ideas
wherever they go, over any kind of terrain, with little real concern
for system. Yet like a Beethoven symphony his myth strikes chords
that ring true in the soul of history. The music of Hoffer's myth
is played on strings stretched taut with compassionate dispassion.
Just as there are two types of music, programmatic and pure, so
there are programmatic and pure forms of writing. While programmatic music and literature represent something beyond themselves,
pure music and literature exist for their own sakes. Seldom does a
musician or writer compose or write a pure form that also points
beyond itself to something higher even than programization can
reach. Hoffer is that rare individual gifted with the vision and skill
to write pure literature that rises of its own merit to the level of
myth.

This means, of course, that no secondary systematization of
Hoffer's thought will ever replace his own writings. Those who are
attracted to Hoffer's myth by this "sampler" of his work should
proceed directly to the primary source, Hoffer himself. There the
"learning" individual will find a true feast.

Chapter Six
American Hesiod

Having been told that he would die at forty, having never attended a day of school, pleasantly surprised by his unexpected late literary success, Hoffer has never lost his sense of wonder at every new day and new idea, his gleeful love of wrestling with new questions, or his conviction that thinking and writing are part of a wonderful game—one not to be taken too seriously.

For sixty years Hoffer has played with ideas the way his "early man" played with toys; and the result is a body of writings that contains a myth of man which must one day be recognized as one of the great political statements of all time. His success lies partly in his "German" profundity, partly in his "French" brevity, but perhaps mostly in his "American" sense of intellectual playfulness. From his earliest books, he has warned his readers not to take him too seriously because he is really only playing with ideas; and since as he says man's most significant intellectual breakthroughs have come when he is pursuing frivolous pleasures, we would be wise to take his play seriously.

With Hoffer's career now nearing its end, we may safely begin the task of evaluating his work and his achievement. It is time to take the first tentative steps in the long process of judging the value, the strengths and weaknesses and sum total, of his myth of man.

The Strengths

Hoffer's myth proves in a number of places extremely accurate and instructive. It provides, for example, one of the clearest and most rationally concise definitions anywhere of the nature of man. Hoffer brought to his study of man few ideological assumptions, except his conviction that everyone, from his early childhood, had been exceptionally kind to him. He simply observed the people around him—in the fields, on the waterfront, in the cities through which he passed—and compared what he saw to what writers before him had said of man. "I'm not a professional philosopher," he has said. "I don't deal with the abstract. My train of thought grew out of my life the way a leaf or a branch grows out of a tree" (EH, 3). From long years of reflection on what he saw and read came his portrait of man as the only unfinished of earthly creatures, the animal that never grows serious, the one that tinkers and makes new things, the one that will one day conquer the very nature that created him. [1]

From observing migrant laborers and reading the musings of French aristocrats, Hoffer came to see how man has always been in the process of building a society in which machines—substitutes for his own deficiencies—would restore the lost paradise he recalls from the days before he cut himself off from nature to become human. He was able to see also that man's greatest enemy, the most formidable obstacle to the achievement of his goal, is his own passion, his "nature within." [2] Hoffer's anthropology serves as a much-needed corrective to all the views of man, theological, philosophical, or sociological, held by spokesmen for a multitude of causes today.

Hoffer's myth also provides a new understanding of the origin, significance, and destiny of man's cities. It is Hoffer who has most clearly explained why the city is man's most natural creative milieu, why men founded cities, what cities mean to them, and the importance of cities for man's future. Cities, Hoffer believes, are inhabited by men of violent and creative temperament. They may be filled with violence and/or filled with creativity. They are never dull. They are man's only hope. City planners would profit by a careful reading of Hoffer. [3]

Like anyone dealing with a society caught up in swift and drastic change, Hoffer has said that change is the central theme of all his writings, and it is certainly one of his major contributions to man's understanding of himself. He has shown us that man is caused by change and not that change is caused by man. Change forces upon man the uncertainty, the insecurity, that either destroys him or provokes him to prove himself by the hard work that leads to accomplishment. Change, Hoffer says, is the catalyst that sends man ever upward. Reaction to change accounts for man's destructiveness and creativeness. For stating this principle so clearly, for illustrating it so forcefully, we are all in Hoffer's debt.[4]

We are also in his debt for his concise, incisive description in *The True Believer* of the dynamics of mass movements and the personalities that originate, lead, and consolidate them. No writer before Hoffer has so well isolated and defined the character of the revolutionary leader. No one has so clearly traced the pitch and flow of events leading to, encompassing, and ending the mass movements led by such men. Anyone who wants to prevent, moderate, or simply understand contemporary revolutionary movements around the world would do well to use Hoffer's books as his guide.

As would the man who wants a "common" man's definition of America. Hoffer's is the best analysis of America's greatness ever written by a man of common origins, outside academia, outside the literary club. For Hoffer America is not primarily its rich soil, its enlightened political institutions, or even its evolutionary history of civil liberty (though he credits each of these) but the stage on which for the first time in all of man's experience the common man has had a chance to prove himself. The common man's archenemy, Hoffer believes, is not the bourgeois capitalist, as Marx would say, but the elitist intellectual who feels he has the right to tamper with the common man's soul. America's greatness, according to the Hoffer description of it, lies in the fact that here for the first time in his history the working man is first and foremost not a worker but a man.[5]

Hoffer's greatest strength, the reason he will be remembered, may be found in his freedom. He has had no intellectual tradition to uphold, no academic respectability to maintain, no image to protect. He has been free to let his thought grow out of his personal experiences and observations the way a branch grows out of a tree. His freedom has made him the American Hesiod.

The Weaknesses

Hoffer's myth is of course not without its weaknesses. A man cannot roam as freely over as much territory as Hoffer has done, without the slightest hesitancy to speak his mind on any subject, without at times stumbling or losing his way. Hoffer has made mistakes, and his myth has its flaws.

For one thing, he freely admits that he studies only the outer shell of most people, events, and ideas. There is little need to dig deeper than the surface of things, he believes, because there usually are no "deeper" truths. This attitude at times makes Hoffer settle for answers less complex than reality may require. What makes this weakness difficult to detect in Hoffer is the fact that his conclusions appear to be the end product of such thorough investigation and energetic reflection. Yet throughout his myth surface reality is taken to be the whole truth about things.

Another weakness is Hoffer's passion to write the perfect sentence, to turn the perfect phrase, even when to do so means he must exaggerate and distort. So great is the pleasure he finds in fashioning a statement with "hooks" for the mind that he will readily sacrifice accuracy for artistic expression. Hoffer would explain and excuse this weakness by saying that his aphorisms are designed to catch in the reader's mind long enough to germinate and grow into something far beyond their original pronouncement. While this is defensible as a method, and a reasonable expectation given Hoffer's skill, it is a bit discomfiting to know that uninitiated readers might not understand Hoffer's motivations or his method and mistake his myth for absolute truth.

Still another of Hoffer's weaknesses, a self-confessed one, one he considers a strength and is perhaps the key both to his literary style and to his acute and unique perspective, is his almost total intellectual isolation. Until his books and television interviews brought him fame, he knew no one who was even remotely capable of challenging his theories. Later, when he could have corresponded and met with his peers, he still chose to work in solitude, preferring his freedom to comradeship. His almost monastic style of life made him what he is—for better and for worse.

In his isolation, lacking formal academic training, finding his books and ideas by accident, his education was random and full of critical gaps. He often had to guess what direction to take from a certain point. An "academic" or "intellectual" environment would not have guaranteed that his work would have been more balanced (indeed it might have blocked his creativity), but it would have given him a chance to debate other intelligent men and benefit from their observations and criticism of his. For example, since Hoffer's work suffers somewhat from his rather superficial knowledge of American history, a free-wheeling historian, one not afraid to deal with mythology, would have made a valuable companion for him. An open-minded theologian would also have been good for him. Yet we must admit that had he been immersed in some "corrective" society he might never have had the gall to construct his grand myth of man, and we would all be the poorer.

Perhaps Hoffer's most costly weakness, which it must be said is in some ways his greatest strength, is his tendency to generalize from personal experience to universal principles. His experiences have been unique for a thinker, and they have given him insights no philosopher before him has had; but his experiences, like those of everyone else, are limited and limiting. He tends to generalize from unique particulars to dangerous stereotypes. He fails or refuses to see the complexities of major historical figures and events, especially when they do not fit his categories. When forced into predetermined molds the way Hoffer forces them, real flesh-and-blood people and their acts tend to be mutilated. There is a great deal of blood on the pages of Hoffer's books. But he glories in his prejudices, calling them "the testicles of my mind."[6]

The Value

When all of Hoffer's strengths and weaknesses have been assessed, totaled, and balanced, there remains what anyone must admit is a tremendous accomplishment. Hoffer's name will live on, not just because of his interesting life (though this is probably what brought him his initial fame), but because of what he has achieved. His books will continue to be read because they identify and clearly state the basic questions men of all ages must ask. They will be read because their answers to those questions, right or wrong, so fascinate the reader that he is inspired to go on in search of his own answers, sometimes far beyond the scope of Hoffer's initial inquiry.

Hoffer identifies the personalities and human dynamics of the passionate men who throughout history have moved the social and political mountains. He identifies the uniqueness of the creative man and the political societies he builds. While his old enemy Marx, another "German" scribbling away in the libraries of an English-speaking country, framed materialistic verities in humanistic categories, Hoffer frames humanistic verities in materialistic categories. Hoffer and his books will remain vital instruments to provoke, to stimulate, to inspire philosophers of the future. He is a grand feast awaiting the enjoyment of his disciples.

One word of caution: Hoffer discourages summer disciples, those looking for an easy journey. At first glance he might appear to be the perfect leader of groups Dwight Eisenhower once called "superpatriots." He can sound as chauvinistic, by jingo, as John Wayne or William F. Buckley. Ecuador commandeers a couple of American tuna boats, and Hoffer would take over Ecuador. He would pin medals of honor on little old ladies who shoot muggers dead. His speeches bring Oklahoma oil men and big-city mayors to their feet with applause. Yet he refuses to wear a necktie or tone down his salty language for society's polite banquets. He advocates and exemplifies a bohemian life-style, complete with commercial nonachievement, for the creative individual. He scandalizes prim aristocratic audiences by saying that America was built by "the scum of the earth," by people who worked hard and made good simply because they had to prove that they were not as worthless as they looked and felt. He is indeed, as the *Christian Century* early noted, the least likely person to be invited to address a local DAR meeting.[7]

Neither has he allowed himself to become, as he easily could have been, the rustic darling of the professional liberal establishment. As we have seen, in the early days of his fame, when "the true believer" was seen as the perfect rendition of fascism's sick threat to mankind's progress, liberals praised Hoffer to the high heavens. He was hailed as the finest product of American civilization, the worker-intellectual, "one of us"—except without the university pedigree. Then in later books and in television interviews, as Hoffer's true beliefs grew clearer, as his acid criticism of "intellectual" elitists grew more strident, his liberal fans began to depart. At last, during the tortured weeks when he served on Lyndon Johnson's commission on violence, he blew the roof off a cozy liberal house-party of witnesses, and the honeymoon was decidedly over. He was quoted as saying that intellectuals hated America and longed for its decline simply because America could get along quite well without them. Misunderstandings multiplied. Hoffer was removed from the list of liberal heroes.

Young people of every sort have always been attracted to Hoffer. They flock to his public lectures. They rush up to stand in his presence and ask him questions. He would seem to be the outspoken but loving grandfather few of them had. He could probably have led any number of children's crusades on any number of occasions about any number of issues, but he has always been honest enough to show young people his impatience with their impatience. He challenges them to spend twenty years "building something" rather than expecting everything to come to them without effort. Though they admire his long exemplary struggle for excellence, their habitual demand for instant gratification turns them away. Hoffer's way is too hard for them.

Even the Jewish community, Hoffer's favorite ("I would fight on the barricades for the Jews."), fails to find in Hoffer a comfortable hero. Hoffer continually praises the Jews, credits them with the creation of Western civilization, says that any nation's true character may be assessed by its treatment of its Jews. He is militantly pro-Israel. But he honestly tells American Jewish audiences that Israel has let them "off the hook" by fighting their battles for them. He reproaches American Jewish intellectuals for their carping criticism of this nation, where Jews have found their best opportunity for peace and prosperity. Once he dampened the enthusiasm of a Jewish banquet in New Orleans by following a long line of fawning politicians to the podium to tell the audience: "They all lie. No one loves you. They would sell you down the river in a minute. Support Israel. It's your only hope."[8]

All of which means that the true Hoffer disciple is one who, like Hoffer, dedicates his life to learning. Only a learner is open enough to the future to be a disciple of the inquisitive case.

Notes and References

Preface

    1. Calvin Tomkins, *Eric Hoffer: An American Odyssey* (New York, 1968). Hereafter identified in text as *"EH,"* with references to aphorisms preceded by #; other references are page references.
    2. *The True Believer* (New York, 1951), p. xiii.
    3. Address to the Boston College faculty and student body, tape recording courtesy of Stacy Cole. Henceforth referred to in notes as "Boston College address."
    4. *Reflections on the Human Condition* (New York, 1973), p. 176.
    5. "Docker of Philosophy," March 29, 1967, p. 38.
    6. From the files of Stacy Cole, who audited Hoffer's seminars at the University of California, Berkeley. Henceforth referred to in notes as "Berkeley lectures."
    7. *Before the Sabbath* (New York, 1979), pp. 1–2.
    8. Personal conversation with the author, 1978.
    9. "Docker of Philosophy," p. 35.
    10. Berkeley lectures.
    11. "Docker of Philosophy," p. 38.
    12. Calvin Tomkins, "Profiles: The Creative Situation," *New Yorker,* 7 January 1967, p. 36. Henceforth referred to in notes as "Tomkins, 'Profiles.' "

Chapter One

    1. This is also aphorism 174 in *Reflections on the Human Condition,* p. 95.
    2. James D. Koerner, *Hoffer's America* (LaSalle, Indiana, 1973), p. 3. Henceforth referred to in notes simply as "Koerner."
    3. "Literary Stevedore," *New Yorker,* 28 April 1951, pp. 21–22.
    4. *Before the Sabbath,* pp. 63–64.
    5. Tomkins, "Profiles," pp. 38, 41.
    6. Koerner, p. 7.

7. *Reflections on the Human Condition,* #179, p. 96 (# refers to the aphorisms of which the text is composed; the book henceforth identified in notes as *Reflections*).

8. Koerner, p. 9.

9. "Literary Stevedore," p. 21.

10. Tomkins, "Profiles," p. 41.

11. Charles W. Ferguson, "Americans Not Everyone Knows: Eric Hoffer," *PTA Magazine,* June 1967, p. 6.

12. Boston College address.

13. *Koerner,* p. 11.

14. Ibid., p. 12.

15. Tomkins, "Profiles," p. 44.

16. *The Ordeal of Change* (New York, 1963), p. 121. Hereafter identified in these notes as *Ordeal*.

17. Tomkins, "Profiles," p. 44.

18. PBS Interview, "Eric Hoffer: The Crowded Life," 1967. Hereafter referred to in notes as "PBS Interview."

19. Koerner, pp. 19–20.

20. *Before the Sabbath,* p. 60.

21. Koerner, p. 33.

22. Ibid., p. 21.

23. Stanford Erickson, "Eric Hoffer: A Profile," *College and University Business,* December 1971, p. 51.

24. *Before the Sabbath,* p. 19.

25. Tomkins, "Profiles," p. 35.

26. *The Passionate State of Mind* (New York, 1955), #188, p. 106. Henceforth referred to in text as *Passionate State* (# refers to the aphorisms of which the text is composed).

27. J. P. Mayer, *Alexis de Tocqueville* (New York: Harper and Row, 1960), p. 43.

28. *Ordeal,* pp. 110–20.

29. Tomkins, "Profiles," p. 52.

30. "Lost Horizons," *Harper's Magazine,* February 1979, p. 16.

31. *Reflections,* #54, p. 35.

32. *Passionate State,* #234, p. 126.

33. Tomkins, "Profiles," p. 54.

34. Koerner, p. 17.

35. Ibid., p. 16.

36. Tomkins, "Profiles," p. 57.

37. From Hoffer's syndicated column "Reflections" (1968). Henceforth identified in notes as "Reflections."

38. "Literary Stevedore," p. 21.
39. Tomkins, "Profiles," p. 73.
40. "Docker of Philosophy," *Life,* 29 March 1967, p. 37.
41. Boston College address.
42. Tomkins, "Profiles," p. 61.
43. Boston College address.
44. Berkeley lectures.
45. Tomkins, "Profiles," p. 62.
46. Boston College address.
47. *Summerhill: A Radical Approach to Child Rearing* (New York: Hart Publishing Company, 1960), p. 87.

Chapter Two

1. Koerner, p. 42.
2. *The True Believer,* p. xiii.
3. Ibid., p. xii.
4. Both as quoted on the dust jacket of later printings.
5. "Blue-Collar Plato," *Newsweek,* 16 January 1967, pp. 92–92a.
6. Tomkins, "Profiles," p. 34.
7. "Eric Hoffer's True Beliefs," 18 June 1963, p. 502.
8. "Hoffer as Historian," 3 June 1967, p. 31.
9. Tomkins, "Profiles," p. 62.
10. Ibid., p. 42.
11. "Dockside Montaigne," 14 March 1955, p. 114.
12. *Passionate State,* #12, p. 12, and #135, p. 77.
13. Tomkins, "Profiles," p. 36.
14. "Man of Sense," 6 May 1969, p. 445.
15. Tomkins, "Profiles," p. 72.
16. Ibid.
17. Berkeley lectures.
18. 15 March 1963, p. 110.
19. "Erich [*sic*] Hoffer: Secular Preacher," 29 May 1963, p. 727.
20. "Eric Hoffer's True Beliefs," pp. 502–503.
21. Boston College address.
22. Tomkins, "Profiles," p. 65.
23. Ibid., pp. 65–66.
24. *Before the Sabbath,* p. 58.
25. "Reflections."
26. Tomkins, "Profiles," p. 66.
27. *Before the Sabbath,* p. 6.

28. "Blue-Collar Plato," p. 92A.

29. "Hoffer as Historian," p. 32.

30. "Work and Days," *Harper's,* October 1978, p. 73.

31. "From the Waterfront," *Time,* 17 November 1967, p. 66.

32. "Passionate Believer," 16 October 1967, p. 38.

33. Koerner, p. 30.

34. "Awesome Epigrams," 9 February 1968, p. 60.

35. Koerner, p. 48.

36. Boston College address, confirmed by correspondence with the University of California at Berkeley.

37. Koerner, p. 48.

38. "From the Waterfront," p. 66.

39. "Docker of Philosophy," 29 March 1967, p. 37.

40. "Awesome Epigrams," p. 60.

41. "Reflections."

42. Koerner, p. 34.

43. From a letter to Stacy Cole, 3 December 1972.

44. *Before the Sabbath,* p. 124.

45. Ibid., p. 4.

46. Arthur M. Schlesinger, Jr., *The Crisis of Confidence* (New York, 1969), p. 19.

47. Koerner, p. 71.

48. Jerome H. Skolnick, "The Violence Commission: Internal Politics and Public Policy," *Transaction,* October 1970, p. 442.

49. Berkeley lectures.

50. "Reflections."

51. Koerner, p. 57.

52. *Before the Sabbath,* p. 102.

53. *Passionate State,* #60, p. 42.

54. Koerner, p. 5.

55. Boston College address.

56. Bill Moyers, *Listening to America* (New York, 1971), pp. 198–99.

57. *Passionate State,* #268, p. 138.

58. From the Hoffer notes of Stacy Cole, 16 July 1979.

59. Koerner, p. 25.

60. *Passionate State,* #235, p. 127.

61. *Before the Sabbath,* p. 41.

62. Koerner, p. 124.

63. *Before the Sabbath,* p. 14.

64. "Bear and Hummingbird," *New Republic,* 19 June 1971, p. 30.

65. "Whose Country?" 13 July 1971, p. 765.

66. "Get Mad, Americans," *American City*, September 1973, p. 38.

67. *In Our Time* (New York, 1976), p. 56.

68. "Bestrides the Narrow World Like a Colossus," 13 August 1973, p. 118.

69. Review of *In Our Time*, *Alternative: An American Spectator*, October 1976, p. 35.

70. 10 July 1976, p. 56.

71. *"In Our Time," New York Times Book Review*, 4 July 1976, p. 12.

72. "The True Questioner," 28 January 1979, p. 27.

73. "Eric Hoffer in His Second Spring," 19 February 1979, IV:4.

74. From the Hoffer notes of Stacy Cole, 1 August 1978.

Chapter Three

1. Public Broadcasting System interview with Jeanne Wolf, "Eric Hoffer: The Crowded Life" (1977). Henceforth identified in notes as PBS interview.

2. Berkeley lectures.

3. *First Things, Last Things* (New York, 1971), p. 12. Henceforth referred to in the notes as *First, Last*.

4. *Before the Sabbath*, p. 88.

5. *Ordeal*, p. 91.

6. Berkeley lectures.

7. *Reflections*, #105, p. 63.

8. "Reflections."

9. *First, Last*, p. 16.

10. *Working and Thinking on the Waterfront* (New York, 1969), p. 82. Henceforth referred to in the notes as *Waterfront*.

11. *First, Last*, p. 7.

12. *The Temper of Our Time* (New York, 1967), p. 34. Henceforth referred to in the notes as *Temper*.

13. "Reflections."

14. *Passionate State*, #33, p. 26.

15. Ibid., #34, p. 27.

16. *Reflections*, #80, p. 51.

17. Ibid., #107, p. 64.

18. Ibid., #77, p. 50.

19. Berkeley lectures.

20. *Reflections*, #106, p. 64.

21. Berkeley lectures.

22. *Passionate State*, #s 18–19, p. 15.

23. *Reflections,* #108, p. 64.
24. Berkeley lectures.
25. Ibid.
26. *Passionate State,* #31, p. 25.
27. PBS interview.
28. *Reflections,* #84, p. 52.
29. *The True Believer,* p. 76.
30. Berkeley lectures.
31. *Reflections,* #87, p. 54.
32. CBS-TV interview with Eric Severeid, "Eric Hoffer: The Passionate State of Mind" (1967). Hereafter referred to in notes as CBS interview.
33. *Reflections,* #86, p. 53.
34. Ibid., #3, p. 4.
35. *The True Believer,* p. 32.
36. *Waterfront,* p. 61.
37. Berkeley lectures.
38. *Passionate State,* #11, p. 12.
39. *Ordeal,* p. 4.
40. *Reflections,* #42, p. 30.
41. PBS interview.
42. *Reflections,* #78, p. 50.
43. Ibid., #102, pp. 61–62.
44. Ibid., #82, p. 51.
45. "Reflections."
46. *Reflections,* #83, p. 52.
47. Stanford Erickson, "Eric Hoffer: A Profile," *College and University Business,* December 1971, p. 53.
48. Koerner, p. 35.
49. *Passionate State,* #271, p. 138.
50. *Waterfront,* p. 28.
51. PBS interview.
52. *Reflections,* #67, p. 42.
53. Berkeley lectures.
54. Ibid.
55. *Temper,* pp. 25–30.
56. *Ordeal,* pp. 86ff.
57. *Reflections,* #142, p. 84.
58. *Waterfront,* p. 124.
59. Boston College address.
60. *Waterfront,* p. 121.
61. Berkeley lectures.

62. Ibid.
63. "Reflections."
64. *Before the Sabbath*, p. 6.
65. *In Our Time*, p. 5.
66. Berkeley lectures.
67. *Before the Sabbath*, p. 123.
68. Berkeley lectures.
69. Koerner, pp. 36–45.
70. Ibid., p. 36.
71. *Reflections*, #109, p. 64.
72. Ibid., #93, p. 56.
73. Berkeley lectures.
74. Author's conversation with Stacy Cole.
75. Walter Lowrie, *A Short History of Kierkegaard* (Princeton, N.J.: Princeton University Press, 1942), p. 14.
76. Koerner, p. 39.
77. Berkeley lectures.
78. *Passionate State*, #182, p. 104; #210, p. 114.
79. *Before the Sabbath*, p. 109.
80. Ibid., pp. 115–16.
81. Berkeley lectures.
82. Ibid.
83. Tomkins, "Profiles," p. 62.
84. *Passionate State*, #186, p. 105.
85. Berkeley lectures.
86. *Reflections*, #92, p. 55.

Chapter Four

1. *The True Believer* (New York, 1951). All page references in Section I are from this source.
2. *The Passionate State of Mind* (New York, 1955). All page references in Section II are from this source.
3. *Working and Thinking on the Waterfront* (New York, 1969). All page references in Section III are from this source.
4. *The Ordeal of Change* (New York, 1963). All page references in Section IV are from this source.
5. *The Temper of Our Time* (New York, 1967). All page references in Section V are from this source.
6. *First Things, Last Things* (New York, 1971). All page references in Section VI are from this source.

7. *Reflections on the Human Condition* (New York, 1973).
8. *Before the Sabbath* (New York, 1979). All page references in Section IX are from this source.
9. Ralph Lynn, Review of *Before the Sabbath, Waco* [Texas] *Tribune-Herald,* 17 May 1979, C:6.

Chapter Five

1. *Reflections,* #183, p. 97.
2. Mayer, p. 92.
3. *Temper,* pp. 1–6.
4. *Reflections,* #2, p. 4.
5. Ibid., #1, p. 3.
6. Ibid., #3, p. 4.
7. *Ordeal,* p. 103.
8. *Reflections,* #5, p. 5.
9. Ibid., #4, p. 5.
10. Ibid., #27, p. 19.
11. Ibid.
12. "Reflections."
13. *Temper,* p. 95.
14. Ibid., p. 45.
15. "Reflections."
16. *Life,* 29 March 1967, p. 38.
17. *Temper,* pp. 95–97.
18. *In Our Time,* pp. 101–04.
19. *First, Last,* p. 36.
20. *Temper,* p. x.
21. *Ordeal,* Chapter 2.
22. *Passionate State,* #60, p. 42.
23. *First, Last,* pp. 122–24.
24. *Ordeal,* pp. 20–21; *Temper,* p. 11.
25. *Temper,* p. 97.
26. *Reflections,* #37, p. 25.
27. Ibid., #37, p. 24.
28. *Ordeal,* p. 108.
29. *Passionate State,* #179, p. 101.
30. *Temper,* pp. 97–98.
31. Berkeley lectures.
32. *First, Last,* p. 36.
33. Ibid., pp. 23–26.

34. *Temper*, pp. 97–98.
35. *First, Last*, p. 33.
36. *Ordeal*, pp. 83–86.
37. Ibid., p. 87.
38. *Passionate State*, #8, p. 10.
39. Ibid., #85, p. 53.
40. *Ordeal*, pp. 5–6.
41. *The True Believer*, pp. 142–46.
42. *Passionate State*, #139, p. 79.
43. *The True Believer*, pp. 146–51.
44. *First, Last*, p. 75.
45. *Ordeal*, p. 43.
46. *Before the Sabbath*, p. 123.
47. *Temper*, p. 87.
48. *Ordeal*, p. 14.
49. *Passionate State*, #104, p. 63.
50. Koerner, p. 101.
51. *Before the Sabbath*, p. 18.
52. "Beware the Intellectual," *Harper's*, October 1979, p. 11.
53. *Reflections*, #13, p. 9.
54. *Ordeal*, p. 40.
55. "Beware the Intellectual," p. 11.
56. *Before the Sabbath*, p. 55.
57. "Beware the Intellectual," p. 10.
58. Koerner, p. 106.
59. Mayer, p. 43.
60. *Ordeal*, pp. 78–79.
61. *First, Last*, pp. 62–64.
62. *Ordeal*, p. 65.
63. *Time*, 17 November 1967, p. 66.
64. Stanford Erickson, "Eric Hoffer: A Profile," *College and University Business*, December 1971, p. 52.
65. PBS interview.
66. Author's conversation with Hoffer, December 1978.
67. *In Our Time*, p. 36.
68. *First, Last*, p. 52.
69. *In Our Time*, pp. 7–9.
70. Erickson, p. 53.
71. "Making a Mass Elite," *Holiday*, March 1966, p. 10ff.

72. From a commencement address at Michigan Technological University, 12 June 1971, distributed as a pamphlet entitled "A Better People."

73. *Reflections*, #36, p. 24.

74. "Beware the Intellectual," p. 11.

Chapter Six

1. For a closer look at Hoffer's anthropology, see *The Ordeal of Change*, Chapters 14 and 15, as well as *First Things, Last Things*, Chapter 1.

2. For a closer look at Hoffer's views on passion and compassion, read closely all of *The Passionate State of Mind* and Chapter 2 of *Reflections on the Human Condition*.

3. For a closer look at Hoffer's views on the origins and significance of cities, see *First Things, Last Things*, Chapter 2.

4. For Hoffer's views on change, see *The Ordeal of Change*, especially Chapters 1 and 2.

5. For Hoffer's view on the common man and the intellectual, see *The Ordeal of Change*, Chapters 3 and 6, as well as *First Things, Last Things*, Chapter 4, and *The Temper of Our Time*, Chapters 4 and 6.

6. *Before the Sabbath*, p. 102.

7. "Erich [*sic*] Hoffer: Secular Preacher," *Christian Century*, 29 May 1963, p. 727.

8. Stacy Cole in personal conversation with the author.

Selected Bibliography

PRIMARY SOURCES

1. Books

Before the Sabbath. New York: Harper and Row, 1979.
First Things, Last Things. New York: Harper and Row, 1971.
In Our Time. New York: Harper and Row, 1976.
The Ordeal of Change. New York: Harper and Row, 1963.
The Passionate State of Mind. New York: Harper and Row, 1955.
Reflections on the Human Condition. New York: Harper and Row, 1973.
The Temper of Our Time. New York: Harper and Row, 1967.
The True Believer. New York: Harper and Row, 1951.
Working and Thinking on the Waterfront. New York: Harper and Row, 1969.

2. Articles

"Automation Is Here to Liberate Us." *New York Times Magazine,* 24 October 1965, pp. 48–49 ff.
"Beware the Intellectual." *Harper's Magazine,* October 1979, pp. 10–11.
"Comments on the Human Condition." *Harper's Magazine,* November 1966, pp. 90–91.
"Get Mad, Americans." *American City,* September 1973, pp. 38 ff.
"God and the Machine Age." *Reporter,* 23 February 1956, p. 36.
"How Natural Is Human Nature?" *Saturday Evening Post,* 13 January 1962, pp. 26–27 ff.
"Leisure and the Masses." *Parks and Recreation,* March 1969, pp. 31–34 ff.
"Making a Mass Elite." *Holiday,* March 1966, pp. 10 ff.
"Man, Play, and Creativity." *Think,* September-October 1967, pp. 8–10.
"The Negro Is Prejudiced Against Himself." *New York Times Magazine,* 29 November 1964, pp. 27 ff. (Reprinted in *U.S. News and World Report,* 28 December 1964, pp. 48–52.)
"The Rise and Fall of the Practical Sense." *Reporter,* 11 December 1958, pp. 27–28.

"The Role of the Undesirables." *Harper's Magazine*, December 1952, pp. 19 ff.

"Some Thoughts from Eric Hoffer." *N.E.A. Journal*, February 1968, pp. 54–57.

"A Strategy for the War with Nature." *Saturday Review*, 5 February 1966, pp. 27–29 ff.

"Thoughts of Eric Hoffer." *New York Times Magazine*, 25 April 1971, pp. 24–25 ff. (Abstracted as "Reflections of a Waterfront Man." *Reader's Digest*, August 1971, pp. 133–35.)

"Thoughts on the Brotherhood of Men." *New York Times Magazine*, 15 February 1959, pp. 12 ff.

"A Time of Juveniles." *Harper's Magazine*, June 1965, pp. 16 ff.

"What America Means to Me." *Reader's Digest*, September 1976, pp. 169–70.

"What We Have Lost." *New York Times Magazine*, 20 October 1974, pp. 110 ff.

"Whose Country Is America?" *New York Times Magazine*, 22 November 1970, pp. 30–31 ff.

"The Wisdom of Eric Hoffer." *Family Weekly*, 24 September 1972, pp. 6–7.

"Work and Days." *Harper's Magazine*, October 1978, pp. 73–78.

In addition to these articles, there are references to Hoffer's syndicated column, "Reflections," which appeared in various newspapers at various times during 1968. There are also references to Hoffer's speech at Boston College, which is preserved on a tape belonging to Stacy Cole; to a file of Hoffer aphorisms kept by Cole during the years he attended the Hoffer seminar at Berkeley; and to Hoffer's commencement address at Michigan Technological University, 12 June 1971, distributed in pamphlet form under the title "A Better People." Finally, there are references to the CBS Eric Severeid interview of 1967 entitled "Eric Hoffer: The Passionate State of Mind" and to the PBS Jeanne Wolf interview of 1977 entitled "Eric Hoffer: The Crowded Life."

SECONDARY SOURCES

1. Books

Koerner, James D. *Hoffer's America*. LaSalle, Indiana: Library Press, 1973.
    A vivid portrait of one side of the Hoffer personality, the salty side, by a man who met him during a somewhat low point in Hoffer's life.

Moyers, Bill. *Listening to America*. New York: Harper's Magazine Press, 1971. A journalist's observation of Hoffer at a San Francisco Arts Commission meeting, one of many episodes Moyers recorded while touring America.

Schlesinger, Arthur M., Jr. *The Crisis of Confidence*. New York: Bantam, 1969. A somewhat gratuitous commentary on American life after the death of Robert Kennedy, quite unsympathetic to Hoffer and his widely expressed sentiments.

Tomkins, Calvin. *Eric Hoffer: An American Odyssey*. New York: Dutton, 1968. A brief text describing an extended visit with Hoffer in 1967, including ample Hoffer aphorisms that illuminate excellent photographs by George Knight.

2. Articles

"Awesome Epigrams." *Time*, 9 February 1968, p. 60. An announcement about Hoffer's new syndicated newspaper column and a prediction about its scope.

Burdick, Eugene. "Eric Hoffer: Epigrammatist on the Waterfront." *Reporter*, 21 February 1957, pp. 41–44. The first serious attempt to organize and evaluate Hoffer's thought, based on his first two books.

Crawford, Kenneth. "Passionate Believer." *Newsweek*, 16 October 1967, p. 38. A comment on the positive effects of Hoffer's first television interview.

"Docker of Philosophy," *Life*, 29 March 1967, pp. 35–37 ff. A pictorial portrait of Hoffer at sixty-five, just before his retirement, with brief running commentary and Hoffer aphorisms. George Knight is the photographer.

Erickson, Stanford. "Eric Hoffer: A Profile." *College and University Business*, December 1971, pp. 51–55. Here Hoffer answers questions about education for life and its potential effects on society.

Ferguson, Charles W. "Americans Not Everyone Knows: Eric Hoffer." *PTA Magazine*, June 1967, pp. 4–7. The first attempt to interpret the significance of Hoffer's life on his thought and especially to speculate on what Hoffer's accomplishment might mean for education.

"From the Waterfront." *Times*, 17 November 1967, p. 66. A description of Hoffer's CBS special with selections from his "salty" comments.

"Ike's Favorite Author." *Look*, 12 June 1956, pp. 40–42. A pictorial portrait of Hoffer at fifty-four with little commentary.

Kemble, Penn. "On Eric Hoffer." *Commentary*, November 1969, pp. 79–82. A reasonably thorough study of Hoffer's life and thought with heretofore unpublished information about his early experiences.

"Literary Stevedore." *New Yorker*, 28 April 1951, pp. 20–22. The first brief effort to describe Hoffer's life and methodology just after *The True Believer* had made him a national figure.

Skolnick, Jerome H. "The Violence Commission: Internal Politics and Public Policy." *Transaction*, October 1970, pp. 436–43. A description of Hoffer's actions as a member of the commission by an unsympathetic fellow member.

Tomkins, Calvin. "Profiles: The Creative Situation." *New Yorker*, 7 January 1967, pp. 34–77. A rich, well-written profile of Hoffer's life at sixty-five, providing biographical detail and philosophical interpretation.

3. Reviews

Berman, Ronald. "Whose Country?" (review of *First Things, Last Things*). *National Review*, 13 July 1971, pp. 765 ff.

Buckley, William F. "The True Questioner" (review of *Before the Sabbath*). *New York Times Book Review*, 28 January 1979, pp. 9, 26–27.

"Dockside Montaigne" (review of *The Passionate State of Mind*). *Time*, 14 March 1955, pp. 114 ff.

"Erich [*sic*] Hoffer: Secular Preacher" (review of *The Ordeal of Change*). *Christian Century*, 29 May 1963, p. 727.

Featherstone, Joseph. "Hoffer as Historian" (review of *The Temper of Our Time*). *New Republic*, June 3, 1967, pp. 30–32.

Gavin, William F. "In Our Time" (review of the same). *The Alternative: An American Spectator*, October 1976, p. 35.

Kirsch, Robert. "Eric Hoffer in His Second Spring" (review of *Before the Sabbath*). *Los Angeles Times*, 19 February 1979, p. 4.

Lynn, Ralph. "Before the Sabbath" (review of the same). *Waco* (Texas) *Tribune-Herald*, 17 May 1979, c:6.

Mackenzie, Ross. "Man of Sense" (review of *Working and Thinking on the Waterfront*). *National Review*, 6 May 1969, p. 445.

Mariani, John F. "In Our Time" (review of the same). *Saturday Review*, 10 July 1976, p. 56.

Merchant, Norris. "Bestrides the Narrow World Like a Colossus" (review of *Reflections on the Human Condition*). *Nation*, 13 August 1973, pp. 117–19.

Oberbeck, S. K. "Blue-Collar Plato" (review of *The Temper of Our Time*). *Newsweek* 16 January 1967, pp. 92–92a ff.

"Philosopher of the Misfits" (review of *The Ordeal of Change*). *Time*, 15 March 1963, pp. 109–10.

Seelye, John. "Bear and Hummingbird" (review of *First Things, Last Things*). *New Republic*, 19 June 1971, pp. 28–31.

Whittemore, Reed. "In Our Time" (review of the same). *New York Times Book Review,* 4 July 1976, p. 12.

Wills, Garry. "Eric Hoffer's True Beliefs" (review of *The Ordeal of Change*). *National Review,* 18 June 1963, p. 502 ff.

Index